P9-DEK-405

The Land of Israel

— is a Holy Land of three religions: Judaism, Christianity, and Islam.
— is the center of the Middle East.
— is the center of attention of the world's concern for peace.

The land of Israel is these things, and more — a land with a rich, complex history. This book explores that history for both the traveler to Israel as well as the thoughtful observer of the Middle East.

Because the story of Israel in the Middle East is 4,000 years old, we need to use both the present and the past to form our perspective of it. What we see is a land fraught with both peril and promise.

This book presents these perspectives with clarity and accuracy. In addition, the books and articles suggested for further reading offer a wealth of information and a variety of opinion.

Illustrating the book are 60 photographs, most of which were taken by the author himself during recent trips to Israel.

DISCOVERING ISRAEL

An Archeological Guide to the Holy Land

by
JACK FINEGAN

WILLIAM B. EERDMANS PUBLISHING COMPANY *Grand Rapids, Michigan*

Copyright © 1981 by William B. Eerdmans Publishing Co.
255 Jefferson Ave., S.E., Grand Rapids, MI 49503
All Rights Reserved
Printed in the United States of America

Library of Congress Cataloging in Publication Data

Finegan, Jack, 1908-
    Introduction to Israel.

Includes bibliographical references.
    1.   Palestine — History.   2.   Israel — History.
3.   Palestine — Antiquities.   I.   Title.
DS117.F52   956.94   80-26952
ISBN 0-8028-1869-2

ACKNOWLEDGMENTS

The author and publisher wish to thank the following for permission to quote from these books:

Follett Publishing Company, a division of Follett Corporation: Alice and Roy Eckardt, *Encounter with Israel: A Challenge to Conscience,* copyright © 1970.

Alfred A. Knopf, Inc.: Emmanuel Anati, *Palestine before the Hebrews,* 1963.

G. P. Putnam's Sons: Israel Goldstein, *Towards a Solution,* 1940.

Random House, Inc.: Marshall Sklare, *America's Jews,* 1971.

The author and publisher also wish to thank Princeton University Press for permission to reprint the following from the author's *Light from the Ancient Past: The Archaeological Background of the Hebrew-Christian Religion,* 2nd ed., copyright © 1959: Map 5, "Palestine," pg. 249; Plan 1, "Jerusalem," pg. 316.

CONTENTS

Acknowledgments   iv
Israel's History: A Chronological Table   vii
List of Terms   viii
List of Abbreviations   ix
List of Illustrations   x

PART ONE. THE LAND: *A Basic Description*   1

I. The Divisions of the Land   3

A. *Historical Divisions*   5

1. Judea   5
2. Samaria   5
3. Galilee   6

B. *Topographical Divisions*   6

1. The Jordan Valley   6
2. The Negev   8
3. The Sinai Peninsula   9
4. Transjordan   10

II. The Naming of the Land   11

III. The Location of the Land   13

PART TWO. THE PAST. *Centuries of Change and Challenge*   15

I. The Prehistoric Past   17

A. *Old Stone Age (500,000-12,000 B.C.E.)*   17
B. *Middle Stone Age (12,000-8000 B.C.E.)*   18
C. *New Stone Age (8000-4500 B.C.E.)*   18
D. *Copper-Stone Age (4500-3100 B.C.E.)*   19

II. The Historic Past: Before the Common Era   22

A. *Bronze Age*   22

1. Early Bronze Age (3100-2100 B.C.E.)   23

2. Middle Bronze Age (2100-1500 B.C.E.)   26

3. Late Bronze Age (1500-1200 B.C.E.)   27

  THE BEGINNING OF BIBLICAL HISTORY: THE MIDDLE
  AND LATE BRONZE AGES   29

B. *Iron Age*   38

1. Early Iron Age (1200-900 B.C.E.)   38

2. Middle Iron Age (900-586 B.C.E.)   39

3. Late Iron Age, or Persian Period (586-332 B.C.E.)   41

C. *Hellenistic Period (332-63 B.C.E.)*   41

III. **The Historic Past: The Common Era**   43

A. *Period of Transition: The Roman Period (63 B.C.E.-379 C.E.)*   43

B. *Byzantine Period (379-640 C.E.)* 60

C. *Arab Period (640-1099 C.E.)*   67

D. *Crusader Period (1099-1291 C.E.)*   73

E. *Mamluk Period (1291-1517 C.E.)*   79

F. *Ottoman Period (1517-1918 C.E.)*   81

IV. **Twentieth-Century Israel: From British Rule to Independence**   90

A. *The Period of the British Mandate (1918-1948 C.E.)*   90

B. *The Independent State of Israel (From 1948 C.E.):*
  A Stormy Beginning   95

PART THREE. TODAY'S ISRAEL: *Its Complexity and Diversity*   101

I. **Its Challenge: Establishing a Just Peace**   103

II. **Its Dilemma: What Is a Just Peace?**   105

A. *The Views of Christian Arabs*   105

B. *The Views of Jews in the United States*   106

C. *The Views of Roman Catholics*   108

D. *The Views of Protestants in the United States*   109

III. **Its Personality**   111

A. *Its Political Structures*   111

B. *Its Political Leaders, Past and Present*   111

C. *Its Working World*   119

D. *Its People*   121

E. *Its Languages*   131

F. *Its Calendar* 131

G. *Its Points of Interest* 132

EPILOGUE. THE FUTURE: *A Time for Peace?*   143

ISRAEL'S HISTORY:
A CHRONOLOGICAL TABLE

PREHISTORY

Old Stone Age (Paleolithic)	500,000-12,000 B.C.E.
Middle Stone Age (Mesolithic)	12,000-8000
New Stone Age (Neolithic)	8000-4500
Copper-Stone Age (Chalcolithic)	4500-3100

HISTORY

Early Bronze Age	3100-2100
Middle Bronze Age	2100-1500
Late Bronze Age	1500-1200
Early Iron Age (Iron I)	1200-900
Middle Iron Age (Iron II)	900-586
Late Iron Age (Iron III), or Persian Period	586-332
Hellenistic Period	332-63
Roman Period	63 B.C.E.-379 C.E.
Byzantine Period	379-640
Arab Period	640-1099
Crusader Period	1099-1291
Mamluk Period	1291-1517
Ottoman Period	1517-1918
British Mandate Period	1918-1948

The period of Israel's self-government began on May 14, 1948, when Israel officially declared its independence.

A note about the designation of eras. You will notice that the abbreviations B.C.E. and C.E. are used in this book. B.C.E., meaning "before the Common Era," is equivalent to B.C.; C.E., meaning in the "Common Era," is equivalent to A.D. These abbreviations are used because they are the ones usually preferred in Jewish publications.

Additional Reading on Israel's History

Baron, Salo Wittmayer. *A Social and Religious History of the Jews.* 2nd rev. ed. 16 vols. New York: Columbia University Press, 1952-76.
Ben-Sasson, Haim H. *A History of the Jewish People.* Cambridge: Harvard University Press, 1976.
Potok, Chaim. *Wanderings: Chaim Potok's Story of the Jews.* New York: Knopf, 1978.
Three major works of historical synthesis, the last especially handsomely illustrated.

Encyclopaedia Judaica. 16 vols. Jerusalem: Keter Publishing House, Ltd., 1971; available through the Macmillan Publishing Company in New York. A completely new work by a very large staff of writers working under Cecil Roth, editor-in-chief.

LIST OF TERMS

Aliyah (ä-lē-yä′), pl. Aliyot (ä-lē-yōt′): meaning "ascent," referring to the Jewish immigration to Palestine

Ashkenazim (ăsh-kė-năz′ĭm): Jews born in Central and Eastern Europe, German Jews, European Jews

eponymous (ĕp-ŏn′ĭ-mŭs): being the person for whom a people or land is named

Eretz Yisrael (ĕr′ĕts yĭs-rä-äl′): the land of Israel

genizah (gĕ-nē′zä): meaning "hiding place," referring to a synagogue storeroom

Gentile (jĕn′tĭl): meaning "belonging to the nations," describing a person who is not Jewish

kibbutz (kĭ-būts′), pl. kibbutzim (kĭ-būt-sēm′): a collective settlement

Ladino (lä-dē′nō): medieval Spanish mixed with Hebrew, the language spoken by the Sephardim

madrasah (må-drăs′å): a combination of mosque and school

mastaba (măs′tå-bå): a type of large, flat-topped tomb in Egypt

moshav (mō-shäv′), pl. moshavim (mō-shå-vēm′): a cooperative settlement

Sabra (sä′brå): a native Israeli

Saracen (săr′å-sĕn): a name for a Muslim used by the Christians

Sephardim (se-fär′dĭm): Jews born in Spain and Portugal, Spanish Jews, Oriental Jews

stela (stē′lå): meaning "upright stone," usually one with an inscription

tell in Arabic, tel in Hebrew (tĕl): an ancient city mound composed of the levels of successive settlements

wadi (wä′dĭ): a watercourse dry except in the rainy season

Yeshivah (yĕ-shē′vä), pl. Yeshivot (yĕ-shē′vōt): meaning "session," referring to the Jewish Academy

Yiddish (yĭd′ĭsh): meaning "Jewish," referring to the language — medieval German mixed with Hebrew — spoken by the Ashkenazim

Yishuv (yĭ-shōōv′): meaning "settlement," referring to the Jewish community in Palestine prior to the establishment of the State of Israel

ziggurat (zĭg'ōō-răt): meaning "pinnacle" or "top of a mountain," referring to the ancient Mesopotamian temple tower built in successive stages to form a pyramid

LIST OF ABBREVIATIONS

BA   *Biblical Archaeologist.*

BASOR   *Bulletin of the American Schools of Oriental Research.*
Both of the above journals are published by the American Schools of Oriental Research, 126 Inman St., Cambridge, MA 02139.

BAR   *The Biblical Archaeology Review.* 1737 H St., NW, Washington, D.C. 20006.

HTR   *Harvard Theological Review.* Harvard Divinity School, Cambridge, MA 02138.

LIST OF ILLUSTRATIONS

Map of Palestine 2
Flock of sheep in Wadi Fara 4
Hills in the Wilderness of Judea 4
Sea of Galilee from Capernaum 7
Hut (with television antenna) in a rocky field above the Sea of Galilee 7
Fortification tower of Neolithic Jericho 19
Chalcolithic temple on the High Plateau at En-Gedi 20
Mosque over the patriarchal grave in the cave of Machpelah, Hebron 32
Jacob's well, marked by an unfinished Greek Orthodox basilica 34
Excavated ruins of Hazor, overlooking the Huleh Valley 36
Roman theater at Beth-shan 36
Canaanite altar at Megiddo 37
Excavating a city of the Bronze and Iron Ages at Tell en-Najila 39
The Pool of Siloam, where Hezekiah's Tunnel ends 40
Roman aqueduct leading to Caesarea 42
Roman theater (restored) at Caesarea, where Herod Agrippa
    was smitten with a fatal illness 44
Mosaic floor in the western palace of Herod the Great at Masada 44
Camp of Silva and the Wall of Circumvallation seen from the
    summit of Masada 45
Synagogue at Masada 45
Replica of inscription of Pontius Pilate's name at Caesarea 46
The Temple in the model of Jerusalem at the Holyland Hotel 47
Map of Jerusalem 49
Early record of pilgrims' coming to the Holy Land, in the Armenian
    Chapel of the Martyrs in the lowest level of the Church of the
    Holy Sepulcher 53
Synagogue at Baram 55
Basilical hall of the synagogue at Capernaum 56

Five-pointed star, later known as the Seal of Solomon,
    synagogue at Capernaum   56
Six-pointed star, later known as the Shield of David,
    synagogue at Capernaum   57
Menorah (seven-branched candelabra) with a shofar (ram's horn) on its left,
    and an incense shovel on its right, synagogue at Capernaum   57
Constantinian floor mosaic in the Church of the Nativity, Bethlehem   59
Mosaic of plants and wildfowl in the Benedictine Church of the
    Multiplication of the Loaves and Fishes, Tabgha   62
Mosaic of loaves and fishes in the Church of the Multiplication of the
    Loaves and Fishes, Tabgha   63
Façade of the Franciscan Basilica of the Annunciation, Nazareth   64
Lower church under the Basilica of the Annunciation, Nazareth   64
Fountain and al-Aqsa Mosque in the Temple area   70
Dome of the Rock in the Temple area   70
Entrance to the Church of the Holy Sepulcher (Anastasis), Jerusalem   74
Moat and wall built by the Crusaders at Caesarea   75
Conically-topped tomb, called the Pillar of Absalom, in the Kidron Valley   76
Franciscan Dominus flevit Chapel   80
Golden Gate, Old City of Jerusalem   82
Damascus Gate, Old City of Jerusalem   83
The Via Dolorosa beyond the Fifth Station of the Cross   85
The Russian Orthodox Church of St. Mary Magdalene, Mount of Olives   88
Memorial of the Holocaust at Yad Vashem, Jerusalem   92
    (Photo courtesy of the Consulate General of Israel, New York City)
Western Wall (Wailing Wall) of the Temple area   97
South end of the Sea of Galilee with the Golan Heights on the far side   98
Arab refugee village in Wadi Fara   102
A moshav in Upper Galilee   120
    (Photo courtesy of the Consulate General of Israel, New York City)
A kibbutz on the shore of the Sea of Galilee   120
    (Photo courtesy of the Consulate General of Israel, New York City)
Street scene in Beersheba   121
Samaritan priests with Samaritan Pentateuch, Nablus   124
Door of a Hajji (Muhammad) in Aqahat et-Takiyeh in the Old City of
    Jerusalem, painted to commemorate his pilgrimage to Mecca   126
Greek Orthodox service of baptism in the Jordan River   129
Bahai Holy Place at Haifa   130
Cave Four at Qumran   133
View of Jerusalem from inside the Dominus flevit Chapel   134
Excavations in the Tyropoeon Valley on the west side of the Temple area   135

Hillside with entrances to the Beth Shearim catacombs   137

(Photo courtesy of the Consulate General of Israel, New York City)

Ornament representing the Ark of the Covenant at the
Beth Shearim catacombs   137

(Photo courtesy of the Consulate General of Israel, New York City)

Administration building, Hebrew University, Jerusalem   139

Dome of the Shrine of the Book, Jerusalem   140

Menorah opposite the Knesset Building in Jerusalem (a gift from the
British Parliament)   142

Note: All of the photographs, unless otherwise specified, were taken by the author; the black and white prints were made by William J. Petzel.

PART ONE

THE LAND: *A Basic Description*

When you think about Israel — as you read about it in the news or the Bible, or as you prepare for a first visit there — you wonder about the land. Is it lush or parched, forested or barren, swampy or rocky? Would you describe it as "flowing with milk and honey"? Would you perceive it that way if you came in from the desert? What is an oasis? A wadi? A tell? Can you see any of these things? How far is it from Tel Aviv to Jerusalem? From Jerusalem to Jericho? From Dan to Beersheba? This book — this section in particular — will answer questions like these.

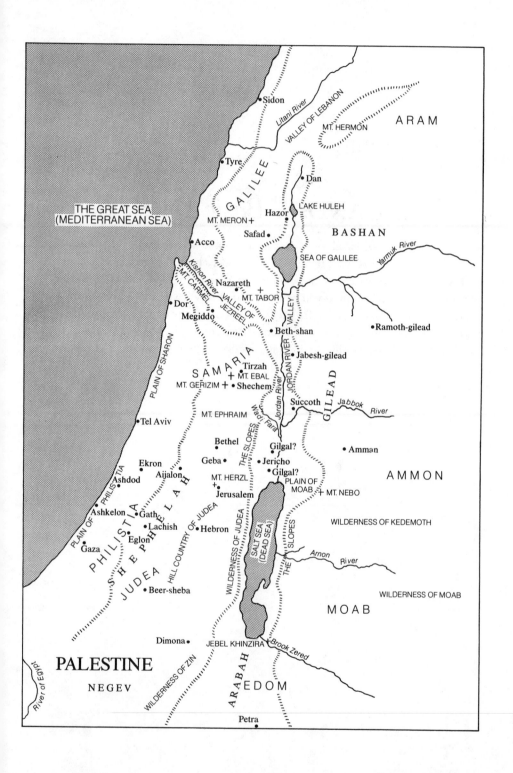

PALESTINE

THE GREAT SEA
(MEDITERRANEAN SEA)

•Sidon

Litani River

VALLEY OF LEBANON

MT. HERMON

ARAM

•Tyre

•Dan

GALILEE

LAKE HULEH

Hazor•

MT. MERON +

BASHAN

Safad•

SEA OF GALILEE

Yarmuk River

•Acco

Kishon River

MT. CARMEL

Nazareth

VALLEY OF

+ MT. TABOR

JEZREEL

•Ramoth-gilead

•Dor

Megiddo•

•Beth-shan

PLAIN OF SHARON

•Jabesh-gilead

SAMARIA

Tirzah•

+ MT. EBAL

JORDAN RIVER

MT. GERIZIM + •Shechem

Succoth•

GILEAD

Jabbok River

MT. EPHRAIM

Wadi Fara

Bethel•

THE SLOPES

Gilgal?

•Amman

Geba•

•Jericho

AMMON

Ekron•

Aijalon•

MT. HERZL

Gilgal?

PLAIN OF

Ashdod•

+

MOAB

+ MT. NEBO

PHILISTIA

•Jerusalem

SHEPHELAH

Ashkelon•

•Gath

WILDERNESS OF KEDEMOTH

•Lachish

HILL COUNTRY OF JUDEA

•Hebron

PLAIN OF

Eglon•

WILDERNESS OF JUDEA

SALT SEA
(DEAD SEA)

Gaza•

JUDEA

THE SLOPES

Arnon River

•Beer-sheba

WILDERNESS OF MOAB

River of Egypt

MOAB

Dimona•

JEBEL KHINZIRA

Brook Zered

NEGEV

WILDERNESS OF ZIN

ARABAH

EDOM

Petra•

I. THE DIVISIONS OF THE LAND

Take a look at the map opposite. (For further reference, check the map found in *Israel Ancient and Modern,* a folder of maps produced by Carta in Jerusalem and published by the Israel Information Services in New York City.) You can easily discern the following features.

Geographically the land is divided into three parallel bands, running from north to south. Along the entire coast there is a long plain, which is broken only where the Carmel range extends all the way to the sea. On the north side of this range the plain reaches inland and forms the broad Valley of Jezreel; at a distance to the south is the Plain of Sharon, famed for "the rose of Sharon" (Song of Sol. 2:1). Running through the center of the country is a range of mountains, which rises to more than 1,000 m (3,300 ft) above sea level. Parallel to it is the Rift Valley, in which are the Jordan River (252 km or 157 mi long); the Sea of Galilee, also known as the Lake of Tiberias and the Lake Kinneret (220 m or 665 ft below sea level); and the Dead Sea, also known as the Salt Sea — the lowest place on earth (392 m or 1,286 ft below sea level). From the Dead Sea down to the Gulf of Aqabah (also called the Gulf of Eilat) and the Red Sea, the valley is known as the Arabah.

Principal cities are scattered: Tel Aviv is on the coastal plain, Jerusalem is up in the central highlands, and Jericho is down in the Jordan depression. Crossing all three parallel geographical bands in the country means traveling a total of 97 km (59 mi): it is 63 km (38 mi) from Tel Aviv up to Jerusalem, and 34 km (21 mi) from Jerusalem down to Jericho. This is the distance by highway; in a straight-line crossing, the distance is only 65 km (40 mi).

A note about lakes and seas. If you wonder why the lakes just mentioned are called the Dead *Sea* and the *Sea* of Galilee, the reason is that the Hebrew and Greek words *yam* and *thalassa,* used in the Bible, designate a general gathering of water, and can mean either "sea" or "lake." The early English translators chose "sea" instead of "lake," and their successors have simply followed their precedent.

A familiar sight since ancient times, sheep graze peacefully in Wadi Fara. They bring to mind Abel, who was "a keeper of sheep" (Gen. 4:2), and Abraham, who "had sheep, oxen, . . . and camels" (Gen. 12:16).

The road from Jerusalem to Jericho descends through the wilderness of Judea, a hilly, inhospitable region. Mentioned in Luke 1:80 and other biblical passages, this wilderness is barren except during the brief springtime, when grass and flowers sometimes brighten it.

A. HISTORICAL DIVISIONS

History has also divided the land into three main districts — Judea, Samaria, and Galilee — but their dividing lines run across the country from east to west rather than from north to south. Though the exact boundaries of the three districts varied from time to time, in general they occupied respectively the southern, central, and northern parts of the country.

In the Bible the land is often described (e.g., in Judg. 20:1) as extending from Dan (in the north at the foot of Mount Hermon) to Beersheba (in the south on the edge of the Negev); the total distance across Galilee, Samaria, and Judea is approximately 225 km (140 mi).

1. Judea

When the twelve tribes of Israel settled in the land, both the tribe of Judah and the tribe of Benjamin located in the south; the traditional limits of the kingdom of Judah were from Geba (north of Jerusalem) to Beersheba (II Kings 23:8), a distance of 80 km (50 mi). In Greek the district became *Judea*, this variation becoming the name of the Jewish state after the exile (Ezra 9:9). The heart of the region was "the hill country of Judea" (Luke 1:65), a veritable fortress of limestone mountains around Jerusalem. The highest point is Mount Herzl, 835 m (2,741 ft) in elevation; Jerusalem itself is 683 m (2,240 ft) high. To the west and south the hills fall off gradually to the Shephelah, or "lowland" (I Maccabees 12:38). To the east and south they descend sharply to the Jordan/Dead Sea depression in a wild and arid area that is "the wilderness of Judea" (Matt. 3:1).

2. Samaria

Ten of the tribes of Israel settled in the north; Reuben, Gad, and half of the tribe of Manasseh settled on the east side of the Jordan. Despite the distance separating them, all twelve tribes came together in a united kingdom under the rule of Saul, David, and Solomon. At the end of the reign of Solomon, however, in 931/930 B.C.E., the ten northern tribes broke away and formed a kingdom of their own. Consequently, Solomon's son Rehoboam reigned in the south, but another man, a former official under Solomon whom we know as Jeroboam I, became king in the north. He resided at Shechem (Tell Balatah) and then at Tirzah (Tell el-Farah), but his sixth successor, Omri (885-874), built a new capital at Samaria, said to have been named after Shemer, the former owner of the lofty hill (I Kings 16:24).

This northern kingdom fell when the Assyrians captured Samaria in 723/722, but many Israelites continued to live there, and settlers were "transplanted" from the East. The city was still called Samaria; in fact, the whole region around it became known as Samaria, too. Its inhabitants, called

Samaritans, were considered a separate group of people, as the Bible points out when it says, "Jews had no dealings with Samaritans" (John 4:9).

Samaria was a good-sized district: it was the whole of the countryside between Judea and the south edge of the Valley of Jezreel. In fact, today it extends 65 km (40 mi) from north to south. Its terrain is mainly hill country like that of Judea, although the elevations are generally not as great as those in Judea. The most prominent mountains are Mount Gerizim (881 m or 2,890 ft) and Mount Ebal (940 m or 3,084 ft) in the heart of the area; and Mount Carmel, which extends for 32 km (20 mi) to the sea, and is 482 m (1,581 ft) high at Zeren ha-Karmel. This mountain is traditionally thought to be the site of the contest between the prophet Elijah and the priests of Baal (I Kings 18).

3. Galilee

Galilee is the third and northernmost historical district in the land. The name means "circle" or "district"; in Isaiah 9:1 and Matthew 4:15 the district is called "Galilee of the nations," suggesting that there were many Gentiles living there — as there probably were, because its northern location and consequent openness to the Gentile world beyond no doubt encouraged Gentiles to settle there.

On the south Galilee is bounded by the Jezreel Valley, and on the north it reaches to the deep gorge of the Litani River, a distance altogether of about 80 km (50 mi). The district is divided into Lower Galilee in the south and Upper Galilee in the north, with its principal centers at Nazareth in the south and Safad in the north. Like Samaria, Galilee is largely hill country, with its greater elevations in Upper Galilee. In Lower Galilee no mountain exceeds 600 m (2,000 ft); Mount Tabor (583 m or 1,929 ft) is the best-known elevation. In Upper Galilee, Mount Meron is the highest summit within Israel's political borders, rising to 1,208 m (3,963 ft).

B. TOPOGRAPHICAL DIVISIONS

1. The Jordan Valley

One of the valley's most remarkable features is great Mount Hermon, which reaches 2,774 m (9,100 ft) and is snow-clad much of the year. On its lower slopes springs provide the sources of the Jordan River, the three headstreams being Nahal Hermon (Wadi Banias), which comes from a high rock wall near the Syrian village of Banias; Nahal Dan, which emerges at the southern foot of the mountain and on the northern frontier of Israel; and Nahal Senir (Wadi Hasbani), which comes from the northwest slope of Mount Hermon in Lebanon.

In its upper course the Jordan flows through the Huleh Basin (22 km or 14 mi long by 8 km or 5 mi wide), where Lake Huleh (67 m or 220 ft above sea level) and its surrounding papyrus marshes have been the object of Israel's major

Variously called the Sea of Chinnereth, the Lake of Gennesaret, the Sea of Tiberias, and the Sea of Galilee, this beautiful lake lies about 200 m (650 ft) below sea level, and is approximately 21 km (13 mi) long and 13 km (8 mi) wide.

A primitive hut boasting a TV antenna illustrates the interesting mix of old and new in Israel. The rocky, barren land surrounding it gives visual emphasis to the parable of the sower in Matthew 13:5 — "other seeds fell on rocky ground. . . ."

Huleh Drainage Scheme. In this project 15,000 acres of excellent soil have been gained for agriculture, but a 750-acre nature reserve has been set aside to preserve the sub-tropical flora and valuable fauna of the region. Below the Huleh Basin the Jordan descends steeply through a narrow gorge and then, in its middle course, passes through the Sea of Galilee. Below the lake it is joined by the Yarmuk River, the waters of which are now almost entirely diverted by Syrian and Jordanian irrigation systems. Finally, in its lower course from Beth-shan onward, the Jordan twists and descends until it reaches its final destination in the Dead Sea.

2. The Negev

South of Judea is the Negev, the name of which means "the dry or parched land." This area forms a very large triangle, with its base in the north on the edge of Judea and its apex in the south at the head of the Gulf of Eilat. In fact, it occupies more than 7,450 sq km (4,630 sq mi) within the political borders of Israel, and constitutes about 60 percent of the entire area of the state. The northern part is a prairie and the southern part is mountainous, with some peaks in the Eilat Hills and in the coastal Negev Hills exceeding 915 m (3,000 ft) above sea level.

As its name implies, the entire region is arid, partly because it has no perennial streams but only dry wadis, which carry water only a few times each year and then only for a few hours. But there are a number of springs in the area, the most notable being Ain al-Qudeirat and Ain Qudeis. In the Wilderness of Zin (south of a line drawn from Gaza through Beersheba to the southern end of the Dead Sea) is Ain al-Qudeirat, which is almost certainly the site of Kadesh-barnea, where the Israelites spent much time during the Exodus period (Num. 13:26, 20:1, etc.); Ain Qudeis is only 3 km (2 mi) to the southeast.

Archeological exploration at no less than four hundred sites in the Negev has shown that early inhabitants of the area developed feasible systems of irrigation, and thus for several centuries prior to 1900 B.C.E. there was settled civilization — towns and villages flourished. About 1900 B.C.E. (at the end of the archeological period known as Middle Bronze I), however, there was a break in the establishment of settlements because, for some reason, the people returned to nomadic life. Only in the Iron Age (beginning about 1200 B.C.E.) was there again extensive settlement in the Negev.

Modern history has repeated this pattern: until only a few years ago, only

---

Additional Reading on the Jordan River

Glueck, Nelson. *The River Jordan*. Philadelphia: Westminster Press, 1946. Explores the river from north to south, and relates the history of the land bordering it. Illustrated.

Bedouin roamed the vast wastes, but now Israel is making the Negev the object of an intensive developmental effort. The National Water Carrier is the central artery of a comprehensive irrigation project bringing water — through canal and tunnel — from the Sea of Galilee to the south, where most of it is used for irrigation in the Negev. Because of this development, and also because of the mineral resources in the region's mountains and in the Dead Sea, new settlements have arisen in the Negev. Of these, the foremost is Dimona, a town with approximately 20,000 inhabitants.

3. The Sinai Peninsula

On the Mediterranean coast the mouth of the Litani River in the north and the Wadi el-Arish in the south are considered the natural limits of the country; the distance down the coast between the two points is 338 km (210 mi). The Wadi el-Arish, usually identified as the River of Egypt (Josh. 15:4), was often regarded as the farthest border of Judah. Below that is the Sinai, the great peninsula which reaches a spectacular geographical climax toward its southern tip in the massive granite peaks of the southern Sinai Range — Jebel Serbal, Jebel Katherina, Ras Safsafa, and Jebel Musa.

Each of these individual peaks has at one time or another been thought to be the mountain on which the Law was given to Moses, the two most often favored being Ras Safsafa (1,993 m or 6,540 ft) and Jebel Musa, the Mountain of Moses (2,292 m or 7,519 ft), both of which rise steeply immediately above the Monastery of St. Catherine. Israeli scholars who have explored the Sinai peninsula in recent years tend to believe that it was indeed in this region that the Israelites encamped at the time that the Law was given to Moses. Consequently, some archeologists find it quite incredible that the Israelites could have forgotten the site of Mount Sinai, because they once lived so near to it and made occasional pilgrimages to the Sinai region.

Additional Reading on the Negev

Glueck, Nelson. *Rivers in the Desert.* New York: Farrar, Straus and Cudahy, 1959. Explores life in the Negev from the Stone Age to Christian times.

Samuel, Rinna. *The Negev and Sinai* (Weidenfeld Colour Guides to Israel). London: Weidenfeld and Nicolson, 1973. A paperback guide to both the Negev and the Sinai, with photographs by Werner Braun.

Additional Reading on Sinai

Albright, William F. *Recent Discoveries in Bible Lands.* New York: Funk and Wagnalls, 1936, pp. 84-87.

Rothenberg, Benno, in collaboration with Yohanan Aharoni and Avia Hashimshoni. *God's Wilderness: Discoveries in Sinai.* London: Thames and Hudson, 1961.

4. Transjordan

East of the Jordan is the land — now the seat of the Kingdom of Jordan —
which was biblically called "beyond the Jordan" (Gen. 50:10) and "the other side
of the Jordan" (Num. 32:19), names echoed by the modern term *Transjordan*. In
biblical times, four main regions, extending from north to south, defined the
Transjordan. Bashan extended for 60 km (35 mi), from Mount Hermon to Wadi
Yarmuk and the Yarmuk River. Gilead extended another 60 km (35 mi), from
the Wadi Yarmuk to the Wadi Zerqa (the River Jabbok). From the Wadi Zerqa
to the Wadi Hesa (Brook Zered), a distance of 130 km (80 mi), was the territory
of Ammon and of Moab, with the city of Amman (called Rabbah by the
Ammonites, Philadelphia by the Greeks) in the basin of the Upper Jabbok. From
the Wadi Hesa to the Gulf of Aqabah, a distance of more than 160 km (100 mi),
was the land of Edom, with the famous Nabatean city of Petra in the red
sandstone mountains in the south.

In all, Transjordan is a great Arabian tableland, which slopes eastward into
the "great and terrible wilderness" described in Deuteronomy 1:19 and other
biblical passages, but on the west breaks off steeply into the Rift Valley. The
Moab Plateau is higher than the Judean hills to the west; at its southwest
corner, above the gorge of the Brook Zered, Jebel Khinzira rises 1,236 m (4,056
ft) above sea level, or 1,628 m (5,342 ft) above the Dead Sea, which is only 8 km
(5 mi) away. Mount Nebo — the place from which Moses looked at "all the
land" (Deut. 34:1) — extends westward from the plateau and commands a view
of the Lower Jordan Valley and of much of the land beyond. It rises 802 m
(2,631 ft) above sea level, or 1,194 (3,917 ft) above the Dead Sea.

Transjordan was always important to the caravan routes which passed
through the region from east to west and from north to south. The land appears
to have been the home of nomads for long periods, though eventually there
arose there the agricultural civilization of the Edomites, Moabites, Ammonites,
and Amorites. Genesis 36:31-39 names kings who reigned in the land of Edom
before any king reigned over the Israelites. Perhaps these were tribal chieftains,
for archeological exploration presently suggests that capital cities in Edom did
not exist earlier than the end of the ninth century or the beginning of the eighth
century B.C.E.

Additional Reading on Transjordan

Glueck, Nelson. *The Other Side of the Jordan.* New Haven: American Schools of Oriental
Research, 1940. Glueck explains what he discovered in his surface explorations of Edom, Moab,
Ammon, and Gilead; he also examines the civilization of the Nabateans.

Harding, Lankester G. *The Antiquities of Jordan.* Rev. ed. London: Lutterworth Press, 1967.

Rothenberg, Benno. *Timna: Valley of the Biblical Copper Mines.* London: Thames and
Hudson, 1972. Discusses recent explorations of the copper mines, and new conclusions about them.

Smick, Elmer B. *Archaeology of the Jordan Valley.* Grand Rapids: Baker Book House, 1973.

II. THE NAMING OF THE LAND

What do we call the land of which we are speaking? This is an increasingly controversial question. But historical investigation shows that the various names were developed and used in an essentially descriptive way.

The oldest biblical name, found first in Genesis 11:31 and many times after that, is "the land of Canaan." The Hebrew name "Canaan" is probably related to the Akkadian word *kinahhu,* which means "red purple." (This term is found in the Nuzi Texts and the Amarna Letters from the fourteenth and fifteenth centuries B.C.E.) It is obvious that purple figured prominently in this society: many Bible passages refer to purple as a very highly regarded color, worn by kings and prominent persons (e.g., Judg. 8:26, Prov. 31:22, and Luke 16:19), and the making of dye of this color from a shellfish found along the coast was a prominent industry. Consequently, the probability is that the name "Canaan" meant "the land of the purple," a name which applied originally to the coastal lands but was extended to include all of the country west of the Jordan. The early inhabitants of Canaan, naturally called Canaanites, inhabited territory described as reaching from Sidon to Gaza and the vicinity of the Dead Sea (Gen. 10:19). When the Greeks traded with the Canaanites, they translated the name "Canaan" as "Phoenicia," from the Greek word for "red purple" (*phoinix*). Thus Canaan and Phoenicia were originally interchangeable names, referring to roughly the entire region at the eastern end of the Mediterranean. Later the northern coast (where Lebanon is today) was distinguished as Phoenicia; the land to the south of that was known as Canaan.

When the Israelites took over the land, it became known as "the land of Israel"; in fact, this name is found in many biblical passages (such as I Sam. 13:19). Accordingly, this is the name used by the modern State of Israel, established in the same land.

Near the beginning of the twelfth century B.C.E. a sea people, whom the Egyptians called the Peleste, moved into the Eastern Mediterranean, were repulsed from Egypt by Ramses III in his eighth year (1177), and settled thereafter on the southern Mediterranean coastal plain. Gaza, Ashkelon, and

Ashdod on the coast, and Gath and Ekron somewhat inland, were their five famous cities. In the Bible the Peleste are called Philistines, and the region where they settled is called the land of the Philistines (Gen. 21:32) or Philistia (Ex. 15:14), a name which was used interchangeably with Canaan, as the phrase in Zephaniah 2:5 proves: "O Canaan, land of the Philistines."

The Greeks, familiar first with the coastal area, named it Philistia, but gradually applied the name to the whole country; in both Greek and Latin, this became the name "Palestine." In this form this name does not occur in the Bible, but it has been used, not only by the Greeks and Romans, but also by the Arabs, Turks, and the British mandatory government, although each may have defined differently the geographical limits of this region. Although "Palestine" may now be a politically controversial designation, historically it has been little more than a geographical designation, usually referring to all of the land between the peninsula of Sinai in the south and the mountains of Lebanon in the north, and between the Mediterranean Sea to the west and the great Arabian Desert to the east.

Of course, because of the events which have taken place there, the land is of special significance to the three major religions — Judaism, Christianity, and Islam. To all three it is a Holy Land; in fact, this designation — "the Holy Land" — is now widely used even in secular contexts.

III. THE LOCATION OF THE LAND

Of all the geographical facts about the land (call it the land of Canaan, or the land of Israel, or the land of Palestine — whichever we will), the most significant fact contributing to what has happened there is no doubt its location at the crossroads of both the ancient and the modern Middle East. If the Middle East may be defined as extending from Mesopotamia to Egypt, then Palestine was and is the bridge between the two. The valley of the Tigris and Euphrates, which was Mesopotamia, and the valley of the Nile, which was Egypt, were the two great homes of empires in the ancient world, and the best route from one to the other lay across Palestine; the sea on the one hand and the desert on the other provided far less desirable routes. Thus Palestine was inevitably and intimately associated with what happened on either side of it, and was often caught in the middle — sometimes independent of the two empires, sometimes dependent on them; sometimes a buffer state, and all too often a battleground.

In ancient history we use the phrase "Fertile Crescent," meaning the verdant curve of land running up the Mesopotamian valley and down through Syria and Lebanon to the Philistine coast, almost to Egypt; Canaan was a part of that crescent. In modern times it is possible to speak of an Arab Crescent, running from Iraq and Saudi Arabia through Syria, Lebanon, and Jordan to Egypt, Libya, Tunisia, Algeria, and Morocco; the land of Israel is in the midst of that crescent, too. Altogether there are twenty-two states in the Arab League. Of these, the ones immediately adjacent to Israel — Jordan, Syria, and Lebanon — are sometimes called the "confrontation" states.

If Palestine is in the middle of the Middle East, the Middle East is itself in the middle of the world — that is, the whole area is at a crossroads where the interests and concerns of East and West intersect. And it is certainly the geographical crossroads of the world. From there it is no longer far to any place in the world: in approximate flying time, from Jerusalem to Athens is two hours; to London, five hours; to New York City, twelve hours; to Baghdad, two hours; to Bombay, six hours; to Tokyo, sixteen hours — and by supersonic transport, half as much time is required to cover any distance. In other words, Israel is at an approximately equal distance from Greece and Mesopotamia, from Western Europe and India, and from the United States and Japan.

Additional Reading about Geography

Anshen, Ruth Nanda, ed. *Mid-East — World-Center: Yesterday, Today and Tomorrow* (Science of Culture Series). New York: Harper, 1956. This book describes the Middle East as the birthplace of world culture and the crossroads of current conflict, the very "navel of the world."

Baly, Denis. *The Geography of the Bible.* Rev. ed. New York: Harper and Row, 1974. An account with references to geology and climatology, but one that is basically non-technical, giving a readable description of the land in general and of its main regions in particular.

Karmon, Yehuda. *Israel: A Regional Geography.* London and New York: Wiley-Interscience, 1971. Comprehensive and authoritative; a highly regarded work in its field.

Orni, Efraim, and Elisha Efrat. *Geography of Israel.* 3rd ed. rev. New York: American Heritage Press, 1971. A relatively technical but immensely informative volume using geological and demographical terminology, and covering not only the regions and climate of the country, but also its settlement, history, and economy.

PART TWO

THE PAST: *Centuries of Change and Challenge*

I. THE PREHISTORIC PAST

There was human life in Palestine in prehistoric times, long before there were any written records about it. But unwritten records of those times remain, interestingly preserved in bones and stones.

A. OLD STONE AGE (500,000-12,000 B.C.E.)

The Paleolithic or Old Stone Age, so-called because of the roughly chipped stone implements which were then made and used, began probably 500,000 years ago and lasted until about 12,000 B.C.E. The conditions of the period are evident from fossilized plants and animals, and from human remains and artifacts. At the time of the Ice Ages in Europe there were pluvial or wet periods, and the climate was relatively moist and warm, but by the end of the period the climate changed — became drier — and has remained much the same ever since. Tropical plants flourished, and wild animals were common — huge elephants, wild bears, rhinoceroses, hippopotamuses, and others. People lived a precarious existence in the open, hunting and gathering their food.

The earliest human traces have been found at a site near Kibbutz Afiqim called Ubaidiya, located in the Jordan Valley on the west side of the river not far south of the Sea of Galilee. Skull fragments discovered here are identified as belonging to Australopithecus, the first erect toolmaker, even older than the famous Java Man and China Man, and previously found only in South Africa. The people appear to have stayed at this spot for some time; when they moved, they left behind their stone tools and the bones of the animals they hunted. Because the bones show no signs of burning, it may be that fire was not yet discovered.

As the climate became more severe, people began living in caves. Caves that show evidence of human habitation are those of Umm Qatafa in the Judean Desert, and Tabun, Skhul, and Kebara at Mount Carmel. At Umm Qatafa, a settlement of the Lower Paleolithic Age, probably established almost 200,000 years ago, there are traces of fireplaces, the earliest evidence of the mastery of fire in the Middle East. At Tabun and Skhul, established in the Middle

Paleolithic Age — roughly 50,000 to 70,000 years ago — there was burial of the dead, an indication of religious thought and practice. At Kebara, established in the Upper Paleolithic Age, about 12,000 B.C.E., there are already more finely made, very small flint implements — microliths — which are characteristic of the ensuing Mesolithic or Middle Stone Age.

In the Upper Paleolithic Age, toolmakers and hunters also occupied open-air camp sites, which have been discovered in protected locations in the Negev and on the Jordanian Plateau. These sites are marked by small circles of stones, usually 3.5-6 m (12-20 ft) in diameter. These probably held down the edges of tents or huts — probably made of animal skins or other perishable material and supported by wooden poles, which have perished, too. Such stones are evidence that primitive hamlets existed, probably occupied for only relatively short periods.

B. MIDDLE STONE AGE (12,000-8000 B.C.E.)

Following the Paleolithic Age, the Mesolithic or Middle Stone Age lasted until approximately 8000 B.C.E. It was characterized by the microliths already mentioned. Most importantly, people were beginning to stay longer in one place and were learning how to grow and store food and domesticate animals. A site of this period is the cave of Shukbah in the Wadi en-Natuf, 10 km (6 mi) east of Ben Shemen in Northern Judea. The prevailing Mesolithic culture, called Natufian, takes its name from this site.

C. NEW STONE AGE (8000-4500 B.C.E.)

In the ensuing Neolithic or New Stone Age, which lasted until about 4500 B.C.E., agriculture and animal husbandry had become a part of daily life, and trade was also familiar. For the most part the settlements were now farming villages of modest size; huts, sometimes partly subterranean, were the common dwelling places. But these humble villages eventually became towns, cities, city-states, and kingdoms. In fact, the earliest cities in the world have been found in the Neolithic Age; of these, the very oldest one now known is at Jericho in Palestine. The rise of cities can probably be attributed to diverse causes, including the pressure of increasing population, the need for security, and the influence of trade.

At Jericho the factors that triggered the city's growth were probably the location, which provided the only oasis for miles on the trade routes, and the great mineral resources in the nearby Dead Sea. At any rate, not long after 8000 B.C.E. Jericho was a city of ten acres, inhabited by an estimated two or three thousand people, and surrounded by a wall of stones set carefully in place on the

Built about 8,000 B.C.E., this massive stone tower and the city wall connected with it protected Neolithic Jericho. The city covered approximately ten acres, and probably had a population of two or three thousand people.

bedrock 15 m (50 ft) below the surface of the present tell. (Some of this wall still remains, rising in places to a height of almost 6 m or 20 ft.) Built against the inner surface of this wall was a stone tower more than 9 m (30 ft) in diameter at the base (still standing and rising to a height of 9 m or 30 ft), with a staircase running down through it.

The people of this time lived in round houses made of sun-dried, hump-shaped mud bricks, and had no pottery; hence Jericho at this stage is called the "Pre-Pottery Neolithic A" city. (About 7000 B.C.E. another group of people inhabited Jericho — at this point called the "Pre-Pottery Neolithic B" city — and built rectangular dwellings of longer bricks, with plastered walls and floors.) By 6000 B.C.E. the people built another city wall, this one of much larger stones than those of the first wall. Of this same date are several human skulls, which were plastered, painted, and given "eyes" with shells inset in the sockets — presumably evidence of some kind of ancestor worship. After abandonment, Jericho was occupied again about 5500 B.C.E. by people evidently unskilled in architecture but skilled in that most important ancient craft — pottery.

D. COPPER-STONE AGE (4500-3100 B.C.E.)

During the Chalcolithic or Copper-Stone Age, which lasted until about 3100

The remains of a Chalcolithic temple pattern the High Plateau at En-Gedi, an oasis that overlooks the western shore of the Dead Sea. The wilderness of hills looming above the site is thought to be the setting of David's flight from Saul.

B.C.E., metal — copper — was first used along with stone. The pottery of this period allows the deduction that the first primitive form of the potter's wheel had been invented, which certainly facilitated pottery production. But mechanization did not necessarily increase artistic merit; often the reverse was true.

Other archeological discoveries are equally interesting. Beersheba exhibits an unusual pattern of settlement in the period in its clusters of subterranean rooms connected by corridors. Tuleilat Ghassul, a site of five small tells in the Jordan Valley northeast of the Dead Sea, is notable for its sun-dried mud-brick houses with wall paintings in black, red, and yellow of human figures, masks, and geometric patterns. Female figurines found at various sites suggest a reverence for fertility similar to the later Canaanite worship of the fertility goddess Astarte, called Ashtoreth (plural Ashtaroth) in the Bible (Judg. 2:13, I Kings 11:5, etc.). Before the end of the period writing is found in Mesopotamia (a pictographic limestone tablet from about 3500 has been found at Kish, and numerous clay tablets with fuller texts from about 3200 B.C.E. have been found at Uruk); thus the Chalcolithic Age is considered a transitional period between prehistory and history in the Middle East, though in Palestine there were not at this point any written records.

Additional Reading about the Earliest Times

Anati, Emmanuel. *Palestine before the Hebrews.* New York: Knopf, 1963. This book explores a substantial part of Israel's history, from the earliest arrival of man in Palestine to the Israelites' conquest of the land.

Hamblin, Dora Jane. *The First Cities.* New York: Time-Life Books, 1973. Describes Jericho as well as Catal Hüyük in Anatolia, Tepe Yahya in Iran, Uruk in Sumer, and Moenjo-Daro in the Indus Valley.

II. THE HISTORIC PAST:
Before the Common Era

A. BRONZE AGE

The period commonly called the Bronze Age began in Palestine about 3100 and lasted until about 1200 B.C.E. In round numbers its main divisions are Early Bronze (EB), 3100-2100; Middle Bronze (MB), 2100-1500; and Late Bronze (LB), 1500-1200. Its subdivisions are as follows:

EB I	3100-2900
EB II	2900-2700
EB III	2700-2300
EB IV	2300-2100
MB I	2100-1900
MB II	1900-1500
LB I	1500-1400
LB II-A	1400-1300
LB II-B	1300-1200

Another name for essentially the same period is the Urban Age, suggesting the change in settlements that occurred during this time. Previously a large walled city such as Jericho was exceptional; now, though many people continued to live in villages and hamlets and on isolated farms, there were many large, fortified towns in Palestine. Many endured for a long time, or were, destruction after destruction, repeatedly rebuilt on the same site. Since each new city was built on the debris of its predecessor, a city mound composed of many superimposed strata was built up, creating what we call a tell. Each walled city was also surrounded by its lands — and by an agricultural people who usually lived outside the walls, either individually or in other settlements. (Phrases from passages like Joshua 15:32 — "cities, with their villages" — suggest this arrangement.)

1. Early Bronze Age (3100-2100 B.C.E.)

Already in the Early Bronze Age major city mounds are found at strategic locations, mounds of cities which controlled main roads and important valleys. An example is Megiddo, a city of the Early Bronze Age which was surrounded by a wall originally 4 m (10 ft) thick and later strengthened to twice that thickness. The site controlled the main pass on the main road — the famous Via Maris (Way of the Sea) — from Egypt to Syria and Mesopotamia, and also guarded the east-west road across the Valley of Jezreel. Beth Yerach (House of the Moon) is another example, an Early Bronze Age city fortified by a wall 7.5 m (25 ft) thick. Located on a site near the outflow of the Jordan River from the Sea of Galilee, it controlled the important road running up and down the Jordan Valley. Archeological remains also prove the existence of a strategic settlement at Jerusalem — on the southeastern hill above the Gihon Spring — about 3000 B.C.E. Jerusalem itself was eventually recognized (under David's rule) as so strategically located that it was made the nation's capital.

Mesopotamia and Egypt. Urban settlements like those in Palestine developed even more rapidly in Mesopotamia and Egypt, and as the cities grew into city-states, civilization flourished. It is interesting to note that civilization and the city are linked etymologically as well as factually: both *city* and *civilization* have common roots in the Greek *keitai*, "to lie down," and in the Latin *civis*, meaning "a citizen."

The Sumerians. The Sumerians were the people most influential in Mesopotamia during most of the Early Bronze Age and in what are there called the Early Dynastic and New-Sumerian periods; they are known for developing the Mesopotamian civilization in its most formative stages. These people inhabited the lower part of Lower Mesopotamia, which was called Sumer — hence their name. They probably invented writing, which developed from pictographs to the wedge-shaped marks known as cuneiform. They also wrote much literature in their language, which was neither Indo-European nor Semitic; they produced remarkable works of architecture (such as the staged temple tower known as a ziggurat) and art (such as the gold vessels of the royal cemetery at Ur); and they developed social and political institutions which were based upon written law. In the valley of the Nile at almost the same time, in what are there called the Early Dynastic and Old Kingdom periods, similar but distinctively Egyptian advances in civilization were made (including the development of hieroglyphics and the building of mastabas — large, flat-topped tombs — and pyramids).

Just as cities had grown rapidly into city-states, so city-states grew rapidly into kingdoms and empires as rulers expanded their domains. In Mesopotamia, probably toward the beginning of the third millennium B.C.E., a certain Etana, the ruler of the city of Kish (90 km or 55 mi south of modern Baghdad), was able to establish control over the whole of Sumer. Not long after that, it is recorded that Meskiaggasher, founder of another dynasty at another city named Erech (160 km or 100 mi farther to the southeast) "entered the sea, [and] ascended the mountains," possibly meaning that he advanced to the Mediterranean Sea in the west and to the Zagros Mountains in the east. It was also about this time that, in the Nile Valley, Upper and Lower Egypt were united under the rule of a single king. This king, whom the Egyptian historian Manetho names Menes, also "made a foreign expedition and won renown."

These developments in Mesopotamia and Egypt would sooner or later involve Palestine; in fact, Palestine might have figured in some of the expeditions just mentioned.

The Akkadians. Though Sumerian cultural influence continued, the political supremacy of the Sumerians was interrupted for nearly 200 years by the Akkadians, the Semitic-speaking inhabitants of the upper part of Lower Mesopotamia, known as Akkad. The founder of this new rule was Sargon of Akkad, who was in power about the middle of the twenty-fourth century B.C.E. He began his career as cupbearer to the Sumerian king of Kish, but soon built his own capital at Agade (probably somewhere in the vicinity of the later Babylon, but not yet found). He united Sumer and Akkad for the first time, and extended his conquests eastward to Elam and westward to the Amanus and Taurus Mountains in Syria and Turkey, thus building the first real Mesopotamian empire. Though Sargon's two sons were plagued by revolts, his grandson Naram-Sin was, like him, successful in major conquests.

The language which came into common use from the time of Sargon onward is called Akkadian, written, like Sumerian, in cuneiform. Much of the literature of the Sumerians was translated into Akkadian; there are many other Akkadian texts and inscriptions as well.

The Amurru/Amorites/Canaanites. In Akkadian the region to the west of Mesopotamia was called Amurru, which means "west." A cuneiform text records an expedition of Sargon of Akkad to Amurru in the eleventh year of his reign, made in order to obtain building material.

The word *Amurru* was also used to refer to the people of the western territory; in its later form, this is the term *Amorite*. In biblical references the inhabitants of Palestine preceding the Israelites — who included the Amorites — were often listed (e.g., in Deut. 7:1) as seven tribes or "nations" — namely, the Hittites, the Girgashites, the Amorites, the Canaanites, the Perizzites, the Hivites, and the Jebusites. Among these, the most prominent were the Amorites, the Canaanites, and the Hittites. Often the basic pre-Israelite population of the land is designated as Amorite (e.g., in Gen. 15:16, Deut. 1:7, Josh. 10:5, Josh. 24:15, and II Sam. 21:2), and also as Canaanite (e.g., in Gen. 12:6, Gen. 50:11; and Josh. 7:9), so the Amorites and the Canaanites may have been essentially the same people.

The Amorite and Canaanite languages are closely related, both being Northwest Semitic dialects. An interesting footnote: Aramean is a language, developed from the Amorite, which used Aramaic and borrowed the Phoenician alphabet; it ultimately replaced both the Akkadian and the Persian cuneiform scripts.

Ebla and the Ebla Tablets. In the records of Naram-Sin we read of a campaign which he made to the Amanus, the Cedar Mountain, and the Upper Sea, during which, among many other conquests, he made the conquest of a place called Ebla. Ebla is identified with Tell Mardikh in Northern Syria (70 km or 45 mi south of Aleppo). The excavation of this site has uncovered a royal palace and tens of thousands of cuneiform tablets, the latter written in an early form of the Northwest Semitic language, now simply called Eblaite. According to the pottery and art objects found in it, the palace appears to have been built during the Early Bronze Age between 2400 and 2250 B.C.E., the latter the approximate date of the destruction of Ebla by Naram-Sin. The cuneiform texts are probably from this same period, or a slightly earlier one.

According to analyses made of these tablets, this city was at this time the capital of a kingdom which rivaled and resisted the Mesopotamian empire of Sargon of Akkad and his successors, and established treaties with Ashur in Assyria. The political boundaries of the kingdom are not made plain, but it is obvious that the areas it influenced and dealt with commercially included all of Syria, Lebanon, and Palestine, and reached south to Sinai, west to Cyprus, and possibly north to Hittite country. Of particular interest is the frequent mention in the texts of many cities in Palestine, including Dor, Gaza, Hazor, Joppa, Lachish, Megiddo, and Jerusalem, as well as of "Ur in Haran." Also interesting is that many personal names used in Ebla are virtually the same as ones found in the Bible: these include Abraham (*Ab-ra-mu*), David (*Da-iu-dum*), Saul (*Sa-u-lum*), Israel (*Is-ra-iu*), and Eber (*Ib-rum*). Another intriguing discovery is that the tablets also contain a creation story and a flood story, the latter reportedly similar to the stories of the flood common to Mesopotamia.

From these discoveries it is clear that, in the Early Bronze Age, Palestine was probably included — as a whole or at least in part — in the western region known to the Akkadians of Mesopotamia as Amurru. It is also clear that many of its cities were already established, a fact evident from archeological finds and from the mention of these cities by name (for the first time, as far as we know, in written documents) in the more recently discovered tablets mentioned above.

2. *Middle Bronze Age (2100-1500 B.C.E.)*

In the Middle Bronze Age Palestine was involved, even more plainly than before, in the international affairs of the time, as we learn from records of both peaceful travel and military expedition in the land. At this time our most interesting information comes from Egypt, where, at the beginning of this period, the Middle Kingdom (Eleventh and Twelfth Dynasties, 2133-1786 B.C.E.) attained renewed splendor after the relative disorder of the preceding First Intermediate Period.

Upon the accession of Sesostris I (1971-1928) early in the Twelfth Dynasty, a certain Egyptian named Sinuhe fled to Upper Retenu. (Retenu was the Egyptian name for Syria/Palestine in general; Upper Retenu probably included Northern Palestine and Southern and Central Syria.) There Sinuhe was received by a ruler with an Amorite name, Ammi-enshi, and settled in his country, named Yaa. The account describes this as a good land, abundant in figs, grapes, wine, honey, olives,ʼ and other produce — a description much like that of Palestine in several biblical passages (e.g., Ex. 3:8, Deut. 8:8, etc.). There is also mention of "the rulers of foreign countries"; this Egyptian phrase probably gave rise to the term *Hyksos,* which means, as Josephus later explains, "shepherd kings."

During the reign of Sesostris III (1878-1843), an inscription of a military commander records that the king marched north to overthrow the Asiatics, and a place called Sekmem fell to him, together with Retenu. Actually, Sekmem may well have been the biblical city of Shechem in Palestine, and because the implication is that it was the center of some sort of rebellion against Egypt, Egypt may have exerted some control over Palestine at this time.

The so-called Execration Texts of the Egyptians, which belong to the closing years of the Middle Kingdom and the first years of the ensuing Second Intermediate Period, are inscriptions on clay bowls and figurines which were smashed in an attempt to magically break the power of enemies. Besides Egyptian dissidents and the hostile Nubians and Libyans, the texts most frequently mention Asiatics; they also name many places in Palestine and Syria, including Acre, Ashkelon, Beth-shemesh, Hazor, Jerusalem, Pella, Shechem, Byblos, and Tyre.

Additional Reading about Ebla

Matthiae, Paolo. "Tell Mardikh: The Archives and Palace." *Archaeology,* 30 (1977), 244-253.
Pettinato, Giovanni. "The Royal Archives of Tell Mardikh-Ebla." *BA,* 39 (1976), 44-52.

In the latter part of the Middle Bronze Age, the Hyksos, apparently predominantly Semitic Amorites, penetrated Egypt, establishing themselves there as rulers for more than a century. Probably occupying Syria and Palestine already in the time of Sinuhe, they doubtless continued to control that land as well as Egypt. In Egypt they established their capital at Avaris on the edge of the eastern Delta; in Palestine their capital was Sharuhen in the northwestern Negev (probably identical with Tell el-Farah).

3. Late Bronze Age (1500-1200 B.C.E.)

At the end of the Middle Bronze Age, Ahmose (1552-1527), first king of the Eighteenth Dynasty, expelled the Hyksos from Avaris and also, after a siege of three years' duration, from Sharuhen. In the ensuing Late Bronze Age the Egyptian New Kingdom attained its greatest splendor: the Egyptians, using in warfare the horse-drawn chariot which the Hyksos had introduced, extended the Egyptian empire to its greatest size. In a series of Asiatic campaigns, Thutmose III (1490-1436), the greatest conqueror of all the Egyptian kings, fought his most decisive battle at Megiddo in Palestine and pushed on to Qadesh on the Orontes River in Northern Syria and Carchemish on the Euphrates. He then established Egyptian administration in the entire country by appointing governors who supervised the local kings and oversaw the collection of tribute.

Later in that period, Amunhotep IV, better known as Akhenaten (1364-1347), devoted himself to remarkable religious reformation but neglected foreign administration, apparently making no response to the many appeals from rulers in Palestine and Syria for help in calming turmoil within and repelling invaders from without. These appeals are contained in the Amarna Letters, Akkadian cuneiform tablets found at Amarna in Middle Egypt, the site of Akhenaten's capital. In the letters we hear of many rulers and many cities in Palestine and Syria, the cities including Acre, Ashkelon, Bethlehem, Byblos, Gezer, Hazor, Jerusalem, Megiddo, and Shechem. Some of the invaders were Habiru, evidently landless, wandering people, known by a name etymologically similar to "Hebrew," but probably not to be equated with the biblical Hebrews, although the latter were at times wanderers, too.

In the early Nineteenth Dynasty, Seti I (1304-1290) campaigned in Palestine and Syria. His inscriptions mention Pekanan ("the Canaan"), Retenu, and Qadesh; he also left a stela inscribed with hieroglyphics at Beth-shan, indicating his presence there. On a wall of the great temple of Amun at Karnak a relief carving depicts the road up the Palestinian coast on which Seti I and most of the other Egyptian kings marched in their Asiatic campaigns. The road, starting from a fortress on the border of Egypt and marked by a line of forts and wells, leads probably as far as Raphia and Gaza. In fact, it is the same route almost always taken by the land armies which have marched from Egypt to Palestine or from Palestine to Egypt.

Ramses II (1290-1224) also fought in 1286 at Qadesh, where his opponents were the formidable Hittites. The outcome was more a defeat than a victory (although Ramses II, once safely at home again, did not represent it as a defeat), allowing the Hittites to advance to Damascus and Northern Transjordan. Some years later (in 1270), a treaty of mutual nonaggression was drawn up between Egypt and the Hittites, fixing the frontier between the two empires along the Yarmuk River. Both great powers were thus weakened, neither completely dominating Palestine; this allowed for the resurgence of local kings and tribes, and for the incoming of the Israelite tribes, whose exodus from Egypt and entry into Palestine probably occurred in the thirteenth century B.C.E., at the end of the Late Bronze Age and on the eve of the Iron Age.

The Alphabet. In the Middle and Late Bronze Ages a strategic linguistic tool was invented in Palestine: the alphabet. Akkadian cuneiform and Egyptian hieroglyphics were both very complex systems of writing. The Canaanites, since they lived between Mesopotamia and Egypt, undoubtedly knew of both systems, but gradually worked out the much simpler system which an alphabet made possible. A cuneiform alphabet of twenty-seven consonants is found on tablets from the fourteenth century discovered at Ras Shamra, but this version did not survive. A version which did survive is a linear alphabet of twenty-two consonants which begins to appear in Early Canaanite inscriptions (e.g., on a potsherd from Gezer, and a dagger from Lachish, seventeenth or eighteenth century). This alphabet was also used for inscriptions in Phoenician (on the sarcophagus of Ahiram of Byblos, thirteenth century), in Hebrew (on the Gezer Calendar, tenth century, and in later documents), and in Aramaic. Both the Greeks and the Romans adopted it as their alphabet, making necessary adaptations.

Additional Reading about the Entire Ancient Middle East

Hallo, William W., and William Kelly Simpson. *The Ancient Near East: A History.* New York: Harcourt Brace Jovanovich, Inc., 1971. A concise, authoritative survey, with particularly thorough descriptions of Mesopotamia and Egypt.

Finegan, Jack. *Archaeological History of the Ancient Middle East.* Boulder: Westview Press (Praeger), 1979. A very detailed study of the ancient world from Iran to Egypt and from Asia Minor to Nubia, with Palestine at its center. Included are many photographs and many references to sources and excavation reports.

_____. *Light from the Ancient Past.* 2 vols. Princeton: Princeton University Press, Princeton Paperback, 1969. The archeological history of the Bible and Early Christianity.

THE BEGINNING OF BIBLICAL HISTORY:
The Middle and Late Bronze Ages

Biblical history begins to include Palestine at the point at which Abraham enters the land (Gen. 12:5). Joshua, leader of the later militant re-entry of the Israelite tribes, summarized the earlier history by saying that their forefathers had lived beyond the Euphrates River and had served other gods; but the Lord led Abraham through Canaan and gave him many children, Isaac and Isaac's sons Jacob and Esau. Esau, who possessed the hill country of Seir (i.e., Edom), was the ancestor of the Edomites. Jacob and his children went down to Egypt; years later, Moses led the Israelites out of Egypt, through the wilderness, and to the land of the Amorites, of which they took possession (Josh. 24:2-8).

Ur of the Chaldeans. Of places beyond the river from which Abraham came, the first to be mentioned (in Gen. 11:28, 31 and Gen. 15:7) is Ur of the Chaldeans. But determining the exact location of Ur is a challenge.

Two facts might suggest the true location. First, the Chaldeans were a branch of the Aramean people who moved into Lower Mesopotamia about 1000 B.C.E. and later founded the dynasty in Babylon, of which Nebuchadnezzar II (604-562) was the most celebrated king. And, second, a splendid Sumerian city named Ur has been excavated at Tell al-Muqayyar in Lower Mesopotamia, a city chiefly famous for the gold vessels of its royal cemetery (from 2500 B.C.E.) and its great, still relatively well-preserved ziggurat (from 2100 B.C.E.). Thus Ur of the Chaldeans could be this Ur in Lower Mesopotamia, where the Chaldeans were later well-known.

It is important to remember, however, that the Chaldeans *were* Arameans, and the Arameans were closely related to the Amorites (the people of Amurru, the "west"); also, the original Aramean homeland was in northwestern Mesopotamia, probably the region called Aram-naharaim ("Aram of the two rivers") in Genesis 24:10. Therefore, the Chaldeans could have been at home there, too — in fact, Xenophon (in *Anabasis* IV, 3, 4) speaks of the Chaldeans as neighbors of the Armenians, which suggests that they lived in that northwestern region. It is also intriguing to note that the Ebla tablets actually refer to a place which they call Ur in Haran (a town today within the borders of Turkey on the left bank of the Balikh River, about 95 km or 60 mi from the point at which it flows into the Euphrates). This city, too, could be the Ur of Abraham.

But there is still another possibility: about one hour's drive from Haran, also in southeast Turkey, is the modern Urfa, which was called Urhai in Aramaic (and Edessa in Greek); this place might possibly preserve the ancient name of this northwestern Ur. In any case, local tradition at Urfa affirms that this was the place where Abraham was born.

Haran. This very ancient city, mentioned above, was probably founded about 2000 B.C.E. In Genesis 12:1 Haran is called Abraham's country. Similarly, in Genesis 24:4, 7 Abraham speaks of his country and the land of his birth, then sends his servant to Aram-naharaim to the city of Nahor to get a wife (Rebekah) for his son Isaac; and according to Genesis 29:4-5, the city of Nahor was close to Haran, if not identical with it. Thus it is clearly possible that Abraham's original home was somewhere in the Urfa-Haran region. (Mentioned in the Mari Texts, a city named Nakhur, situated east of the Upper Balikh River, may be this same city.) Later Jacob also went to Haran (Gen. 27:43), where he married Leah and Rachel, and where all of his sons except Benjamin were born (Gen. 29:32-30:24). He himself was remembered as "a wandering Aramean" (Deut. 26:5). Thus Abraham, Isaac, and Jacob — the fathers (or patriarchs, as they were called in Greek, according to Acts 7:8) — and the twelve sons of Jacob (the ancestors of the twelve tribes of Israel) had close connections with the Upper Euphrates region.

A Note on the Family Relationships of the Israelite Tribes. Genesis 10 pictures humankind as a family descended from Shem, Ham, and Japheth: the three sons of Noah born to him after the flood were the ancestors of the Semitic, Hamitic, and Japhetic peoples. In the line of descent from Shem is Eber, the ancestor of the Hebrews, from whom they take their name; and in the line of Eber (Gen. 11:16ff.) is Terah, who was the father of Abram or Abraham (the name occurs in both forms), Nahor, and Haran. Haran died in Ur, but left a son, Lot, and two daughters, Milcah and Iscah. Abraham married Sarai (Sarah), and his brother Nahor married Milcah, who was the daughter of the other brother, Haran. The son of Abraham and Sarah was Isaac (Gen. 21:3).

The last of a number of sons of Nahor and Milcah was Bethuel (Gen. 22:22), who was the father of Laban and Rebekah (Gen. 24:24, 29). Isaac married Rebekah (Gen. 24:67); the two were the parents of Esau and Jacob (Gen. 25:25-26). Laban's daughters were Leah and Rachel, who became the wives of Jacob. They and their maids became the mothers of the twelve sons of Jacob. (The sons of Leah were Reuben, Simeon, Levi, Judah, Issachar, and Zebulun; the sons of Bilhah, Rachel's maid, were Dan and Naphtali; the sons of

---

Additional Reading on the Ur of Abraham

Gordon, Cyrus H. "Where Is Abraham's Ur?" *BAR,* 3 (1977), 20ff. Notes that Tell al-Muqayyar is never called "Ur of the Chaldeans" in ancient sources, and argues that Abraham's Ur is located in northwest Mesopotamia.

Parrot, André. *Abraham and His Times.* Philadelphia: Fortress Press, 1968. Proposes that Abraham came from the Sumerian Ur in Lower Mesopotamia, and identifies him as a Semite of the Aramean branch.

Zilpah, Leah's maid, were Gad and Asher; and the sons of Rachel were Joseph and Benjamin.) Since Jacob also received the name of Israel (Gen. 32:28), these were the children of Israel.

Abraham in Canaan. When Abraham came from Ur and Haran into Canaan, he pitched his tent and built altars to the Lord at various places from Shechem to Hebron (Gen. 12-13). Later, by agreement with Abimelech, Philistine king of Gerar (Gen. 26:1), he dug a well and planted a tamarisk tree at Beersheba (Gen. 21:30, 33). Finally, at Hebron he purchased a burying place for his wife Sarah (Gen. 23): the field of Ephron the Hittite, with the cave of Machpelah at the end of the field. Eventually he himself (Gen. 25:9), Isaac and Rebekah, and Jacob and Leah were also buried there (Gen. 25:9; 49:29-31; 50:13).

A Note on the Philistines and the Hittites. Other than in the story of Abraham, we hear of the Philistines only in writings of about 1200 B.C.E., but perhaps there were a like people who also came into Palestine from the Aegean at an earlier time. As for the Hittites, their great kingdom flourished in Anatolia from about 1700 to 1200 B.C.E., but Hittite names of persons and places are found as early as 2000 B.C.E. in Old Assyrian inscriptions from Cappadocia, and there seems to be no reason why there could not have been Hittites living in Palestine in the time of Abraham. In fact, details in the account of Abraham's purchase of the field of Ephron correspond to details of legal practice denoted in later Hittite documents found at their capital of Boghazköy in Asia Minor.

Abraham Remembered. In his time Herod the Great built an imposing enclosure around the site of the cave of Machpelah, with walls about 2.5 m (8 ft) thick, which are still to be seen at Hebron. In the Byzantine period (probably in the mid-fifth century) a church was built within the enclosure. After the Arab conquest of Palestine this was converted into a mosque, under the Crusaders it was rebuilt as a church, and after the Crusaders left the place again became a mosque, which it is today. The Arabic name for it is the Haram el-Khalil, "the sacred precinct of the Friend," and Hebron itself is also called el-Khalil, "the Friend," both names recalling the designation of Abraham as the friend of God (in II Chron. 20:7, Isa. 41:8, and James 2:23).

As these references indicate, Abraham has always been remembered by Christians and Muslims, as well as by Jews, as an outstanding person in the

---

Additional Reading on the Philistines and Hittites at the Time of Abraham

Kitchen, K. A. *Ancient Orient and Old Testament.* London: Tyndale Press, 1966, pp. 80f.
Lehmann, Manfred R. "Abraham's Purchase of Machpelah and Hittite Law." *BASOR,* 129 (1953), 15-18.

A modern mosque marks the patriarchal grave in the cave of Machpelah in Hebron. In it are the cenotaphs of Abraham and Sarah, Isaac and Rebekah, and Jacob and Leah, which presumably mark the actual tombs in the cave below.

history of religion. Paul cites Abraham as an example in his argument concerning justification by faith (Rom. 4:1-12), and the Letter to the Hebrews names Abraham as one of the heroes of the faith, who still constitute a great cloud of witnesses. In the Koran Muhammad declares that "Abraham was neither Jew nor Christian; but he was sound in the faith, a Muslim" (Surah III, 60). Muhammad also believed, apparently, that the son whom Abraham almost sacrificed was not Isaac but Ishmael, whose mother was Hagar, the Egyptian handmaid of Sarah (Surah XXXVII, 99-110). He indicates that Abraham and Ishmael were the founders of the cult of the Kaabah at Mecca (Surah II, 119), claiming Ishmael was an apostle and a prophet (Surah XIX, 55). Thus Abraham and Ishmael are considered forefathers of the Arabs.

Isaac. Like Abraham, Isaac had dealings with Abimelech, king of Gerar. In his land Isaac sowed crops very successfully and re-dug the wells which had originally been dug in Abraham's time. Isaac's herdsmen and the herdsmen of

Gerar argued about who owned two of the wells, and Isaac gave in to the latter. But a third well was his without contention, and he called it Rehoboth, meaning "broad places," and said, "For now the Lord has made room for us, and we shall be fruitful in the land" (Gen. 26:17-22). Ancient Rehoboth is now Ruheibeh, 30 km (19 mi) southwest of Beersheba. Notable there are the several large cisterns of Byzantine date, probably similar to those the partriarchs dug in the rock in their day.

Jacob. When Jacob returned from Haran, where he spent so many years working for his uncle Laban the Aramean (Gen. 29:10; 31:20), he built a house at Succoth (Gen. 33:17). This site, identified as Tell Deiralla in Transjordan, is 3 km (2 mi) north of the River Jabbok (Wadi Zerqa), where he had received the name Israel (Gen. 32:28). Thereafter he crossed the Jordan and pitched his tent at Shechem (identical with Tell Balatah), then purchased from the sons of Hamor, Shechem's father, the land where he had camped (Gen. 33:18-19). Later, Jacob's sons pastured their father's flock in the vicinity of Shechem and northward to Dothan (Gen. 37:12-17), the latter identified as Tell Dotha.

Jacob's life in Shechem was marked by a few violent incidents. An unhappy event was the rape of Dinah (daughter of Jacob and Leah) by Shechem, son of Hamor, in retaliation for which Simeon and Levi attacked the city and killed both Hamor and Shechem (Gen. 34). Also, shortly before his death, Jacob said that he was giving to Joseph a "shoulder" (probably Shechem, which is on the mountain slopes or "shoulders" of Mount Gerizim and Mount Ebal) which he had taken from the Amorites with his sword and bow (Gen. 48:22). Otherwise, however, Jacob appears to have maintained generally peaceful relations with the Canaanites of the Shechem area.

In fact, the plot of land that Jacob bought at Shechem eventually provided the burial place for his son Joseph, whose body was originally embalmed in Egypt and then brought to Palestine by the people of Israel at the time of the Exodus (Gen. 50:26; Josh. 24:32). Jacob also apparently built the well near the field he gave to Joseph. About it the Samaritan woman later said to Jesus that "our father Jacob . . . gave us the well" (John 4:12); and Jews, Christians, and Muslims today recognize it as Jacob's well. A church was built around the well in the fourth century C.E., and rebuilt by the Crusaders; there is today an unfinished Greek Orthodox basilica on the site.

A Note on the Dates of the Patriarchs and of the Exodus. According to the biblical chronology, Abraham was 75 years old when he left Haran (Gen. 12:4) and 100 years old when Isaac was born (Gen. 21:5). Isaac was 60 years old when Jacob was born (Gen. 25:26), and Jacob was 130 years old when he went down to Egypt (Gen. 47:9). Therefore, the span from Abraham's coming to Canaan to

The massive walls of an unfinished Greek Orthodox basilica seem to stand guard over Jacob's well. A subterranean room encloses the mouth of the well, which is surrounded by a massive stone curb about 2.2 m (7½ ft) in diameter. Now about 26 m (85 ft) deep, the well was originally deeper.

Jacob's going to Egypt was 215 years. According to Exodus 12:40, in the Hebrew and Greek texts, the children of Israel were in Egypt either 215 or 430 years until the Exodus.

Estimations of the date of the Exodus vary. It may have occurred in the fifteenth century, 480 years before Solomon began to build the temple — mentioned in I Kings 6:1 — in the fourth year of his reign, about 967/966 B.C.E. (a date thus occurring during the reign of Thutmose III, 1490-1436). Or it may have occurred in the fourteenth century (because of the supposed similarity of the teaching of Moses to the monotheism of Akhenaten, 1364-1347); or in the thirteenth century (because the Israelites built the store city of Ramses II, 1290-1224, and because Merneptah, 1224-1204, says he defeated Israel in Canaan). The thirteenth-century date is the one most likely correct — one that would place Abraham in the nineteenth or seventeenth century B.C.E., the nineteenth being the more probable choice (according to the Hebrew text of Exodus 12:40, which indicates that the sojourn of the Israelites in Egypt lasted for 430 years).

Moses. As the leader of the Exodus, Moses is considered the greatest prophet in Jewish history (Deut. 34:10). He taught that there is only one God, who cannot be seen, who must not be represented in any form, and who is the source of justice. Basically he taught monotheism, augmented by a system of social and religious laws. In their developed form in the first five books of the Bible, these are known as the Law of Moses or the Torah; they outline an entire way of life, with a strong emphasis upon social justice and the relief of misery.

Joshua. After Moses died and was buried on the east side of the Jordan (Deut. 34:6), his successor, Joshua, led the Israelite tribes in their return to the land of Canaan (Deut. 31:7), the story of which is told in the Book of Joshua. Unlike their forefathers, who lived relatively peacefully in the midst of the Canaanites (indicated by the ideal of Rehoboth, meaning "broad places," with room enough for all), the Israelites were frequently at war. Jericho was taken; Gibeon capitulated; five Amorite kings led by Adonizedek, king of Jerusalem,

---

Additional Reading on Abraham and the Patriarchs

Pfeiffer, Charles F. *The Patriarchal Age.* Grand Rapids: Baker Book House, 1961. Considers the patriarchs as men — ordinary in many ways — living in a real world known through archeological research. Their daily life and their theology are among the topics covered.

Additional Reading on Moses

Albright, William F. *From the Stone Age to Christianity: Monotheism and the Historical Process.* 2nd ed. Garden City: Doubleday, Anchor Books, 1957, pp. 254-272. The famous archeologist strongly affirms that Moses was a monotheist.

Beegle, Dewey M. *Moses, The Servant of Yahweh.* Grand Rapids: Eerdmans, 1972. Moses is described as the founder of the community of Israel, and his greatness ascribed to his personal relationship with God.

Daiches, David. *Moses: The Man and His Vision.* New York: Praeger, 1975. As defined in this book, the Mosaic tradition emphasized the absoluteness of the power of Yahweh, the absolute nature of his ethical demands, and the special character of the relationship he established with Israel.

Pearlman, Moshe. *Moses: Where It All Began.* New York: Abelard-Schuman, 1974. A handsome presentation of the life and work of Moses, with photographs by David Harris.

The ruins of Hazor are rich in history. Excavators have uncovered more than twenty strata of occupation, from the Early Bronze Age to the Hellenistic period. Though destroyed in the latter half of the thirteenth century B.C.E. (Stratum XIII), the city became relatively prosperous again by Solomon's time (Stratum X).

This Roman theater is one of numerous archeological discoveries at Beth-shan, which occupied a strategic location at the junction of the Valley of Jezreel and the Jordan Valley. Beth-shan's eighteen archeological strata date from 3500 B.C.E. to the Hellenistic and Roman periods (when the city was named Scythopolis).

attacked Gibeon but were routed and killed; southern cities, including Lachish and Debir, were smitten; and in the north, Hazor, head of a coalition of five kingdoms, was taken.

The record of Joshua's taking of Hazor is typical: "And they put to the sword all who were in it, utterly destroying them; there was none left that breathed, and he burned Hazor with fire" (Josh. 11:11). It was said (e.g., in Josh. 6:17) that the cities were "devoted [*herem*] to the Lord for destruction," a destruction defended as necessary to prevent the Canaanites from teaching the Israelites "to do according to all their abominable practices which they have done in the service of their gods" (Deut. 20:16-18). However, of "the cities that stood on mounds" (i.e., the great fortified Canaanite cities on their tells), only Hazor was destroyed (Josh. 11:13); such cities as Beth-shan, Taanach, and Megiddo were not taken. Supporting this conclusion is the discovery of burned layers at such cities as Lachish, Debir, and Hazor, which probably date back to the latter half of the thirteenth century and may probably be attributed to the Israelite

Framed by date palms is this Canaanite altar at Megiddo. Like Beth-shan, Megiddo was a strategic city, commanding a view of the pass overlooking the Valley of Jezreel (the Plain of Esdraelon). It was occupied from Stratum XX (mid-fourth millennium B.C.E.) to Stratum I of the Persian period.

conquest, whereas Megiddo and other sites show evidence of continuing Canaanite culture.

B. IRON AGE

1. Early Iron Age (1200-900 B.C.E.)

Judges. In the next two centuries (the twelfth and eleventh) the Israelite tribes gradually consolidated themselves in Canaan. Although relatively isolated in various parts of the land, the tribes occasionally were loosely united — particularly in dangerous times — under leaders called "judges," whose exploits are narrated in the Book of Judges. Those against whom they fought included not only the Canaanites but also the Ammonites in Transjordan, the Midianites who invaded the Jezreel Valley, and the Philistines who were settled on the southern coast. Famous "judges" who were actually military leaders included Deborah, Gideon, Jephthah, and Samson; Samuel was actually a true judge, an administrator of justice (I Sam. 7:15).

The Kingdom United; the First Temple. Finally a more closely united kingdom was established under the broader and more stable rule of the first kings: Saul, David, and Solomon. Saul checked the penetration of the Philistines, although he died in a last battle against them (I Sam. 31). David gained victories over enemies on all sides, and established the capital at Jerusalem, which he took from the Jebusites. This city provided him an ideally neutral place from which to rule all the tribes, since it had not previously belonged to any of them. Solomon accomplished much — he built the Temple on Mount Moriah (II Chron. 3:1), for example. But all his projects placed a heavy burden of taxes and forced labor upon the people, which led to the division of the kingdom.

Additional Reading on the Canaanites

Albright, William F. *The Archaeology of Palestine.* Harmondsworth, England: Penguin Books, 1949. Explains how the Canaanites exhausted their cultural energy, then points out that "after a long eclipse and a fresh transfusion of blood they were to emerge as a vital new people, the Phoenicians, who shared with Israel the material achievements of Iron Age Palestine" (p. 109).

Anati, Emmanuel. *Palestine before the Hebrews.* New York: Knopf, 1963. Studies the cult figurines found in Palestine and the religious texts discovered at Ras Shamra (ancient Ugarit, 14th-15th centuries B.C.E.), and draws an interesting conclusion: "Human sacrifice, which had been given up long before by the people of Mesopotamia and Egypt, was still in current use in Canaan.... Serpent worship and the concepts suggested by their ruthless divinities, who were framed in a mythology full of atrocity, fear, and brutality, were most likely reflections of the facts and rules of daily life" (p. 427).

Gray, John. *The Canaanites* (Ancient Peoples and Places Series). London: Thames and Hudson, 1964. Describes the daily life of the Canaanites, quotes extensively from the Ras Shamra texts, and pictures Canaanite objects of art. Many positive factors of Canaanite culture are noted, including what the author calls their greatest contribution to human progress — the alphabet.

Excavators work carefully on the site of an old city at Tell en-Najila, one of the largest mounds in southern Palestine. Though the identification of the site is uncertain, it has fourteen archeological strata, and has yielded the most important remains of the Bronze and Iron Ages (Strata XIII-III).

2. Middle Iron Age (900-586 B.C.E.)

The Divided Kingdom and the Exile. After Solomon's death, the northern tribes, led by Jeroboam I, successfully revolted and established the Northern Kingdom, a fateful division of the previously united realms that occurred about 931/930 B.C.E. The northern capital was successively at Shechem and at Tirzah under Jeroboam I; later, from the reign of Omri onward, it was established at Samaria. In 732 B.C.E. Tiglath-pileser III conquered many places in Northern Israel and carried off many captives to Assyria (II Kings 15:29). In 722 Shalmaneser V took Samaria after a three-year siege and took captive to Assyria the remaining Israelites, an event that marked the end of the Northern Kingdom.

The Southern Kingdom continued at Jerusalem under Rehoboam, son of Solomon, and his successors. Sennacherib of Assyria threatened Jerusalem in the time of King Hezekiah (701 B.C.E.), a threat which probably led to the construction of Hezekiah's Tunnel and of additional city walls, but it was only the Chaldeans (New Babylonians) who brought an end to the kingdom. In 597 B.C.E. Nebuchadnezzar II captured Jerusalem and took into captivity to Babylon King Jehoiachin and all except the poorest people of the land (II Kings 24:14-16); again in 586 he conquered and burned the city and took many more people captive. Living during these and later times were the great Hebrew prophets, who proclaimed their ideals of justice, kindness, and universal peace (e.g., in Mic. 6:8, Isa. 2:4). The full narrative of these times is found in the books of Kings and Chronicles.

Bright sunshine highlights the Pool of Siloam, where Hezekiah's Tunnel ends. Because the tunnel was dug to bring water into Jerusalem when it was besieged, the pool must have been inside the city walls at that time. In the fifth century C.E. the Empress Eudocia built a Byzantine church here.

3. Late Iron Age, or Persian Period (586-332 B.C.E.)

The Synagogue and the Academy. In Babylonia the Jewish exiles — bereft of their Temple in Jerusalem — developed a new institution very important to their

---

Additional Reading on Israel, the Kings, and the Prophets

de Vaux, Roland. *Ancient Israel: Its Life and Institutions.* New York: McGraw-Hill, 1961. Detailed discussion of the family, the state, and cults in Israel from tribal to post-exilic times.

Pearlman, Moshe. *In the Footsteps of the Prophets.* New York: Crowell, 1975. Like the author's *Moses,* a handsomely illustrated account, with photographs by David Harris.

Thiele, Edwin R. *A Chronology of the Hebrew Kings.* Grand Rapids: Zondervan, 1977. Based upon earlier, more extensive studies, this is a condensed and simplified presentation of the problems of correctly determining biblical chronology during the time of the kings, and the solutions to these problems. The included table of the dates of the kings of Judah and of Israel is widely regarded as the most nearly correct table presently attainable.

religious future: the synagogue. When they returned to Palestine, they not only rebuilt the Temple, but they also instituted the synagogue as a place of religious assembly. When the Temple was again destroyed, the synagogue provided a continuing place of worship which could be established wherever there was a community of Jews. In Hebrew it was called Beth Tephila (House of Prayer), Beth Hamidrash (House of Study), and Beth Haknesset, meaning "house of assembly," the abbreviated term *Knesset* now being the name of the parliament of Israel. In time the synagogue provided a pattern for both the Christian church and the Muslim mosque.

Another institution of great importance was the Academy, or *Yeshivah* in Hebrew, meaning "a sitting or session." This Academy, which became the chief place of advanced study, was found in Babylonia, Palestine, and many other places where there were communities of Jews.

Return from Exile. In 539 the Persian ruler Cyrus II took Babylon, and in his first year of reign at Babylon (538/537) issued a decree allowing the exiles to return to their homeland (II Chron. 36:22, 23; Ezra 1:1-4). A descendant of David was allowed to serve as governor of those who returned, but could not be called king. (The last king had been Jehoiachin, who lived in exile after being taken captive to Babylon in 597 B.C.E.) At first Sheshbazzar, and later Zerubbabel (the "scion of Babylon," a grandson of Jehoiachin), acted as governors.

The Second Temple. Under Darius I (521-486) the prophets Haggai and Zechariah encouraged the rebuilding of the Temple, a task completed in 516/515 B.C.E. (Ezra 6:15), seventy years after the destruction of the first Temple (Jer. 29:10). Under Artaxerxes — probably Artaxerxes I (464-424) — Ezra and Nehemiah also came back to Jerusalem, and Nehemiah led in the rebuilding of the walls of the city.

C. HELLENISTIC PERIOD (332-63 B.C.E.)

The period of the second Temple lasted until 70 C.E., when the second Temple, like the first, was destroyed. Within this period the Jews lived at first under Persian supremacy; then, after the conquest of the entire Middle East by Alexander the Great (332 B.C.E.), they lived under Hellenistic rule. In 168 B.C.E. Antiochus IV Epiphanes, the ruler of Syria, attempted the Hellenization of the Jews and thereby provoked the amazingly successful Maccabean revolt, which made Judah completely independent once again. Judah was then ruled by the Hasmonean (or Maccabean) dynasty, but two rivals to the throne invited the Roman general Pompey to settle their dispute, and thus the country came under the control of the Romans (63 B.C.E.).

This elevated aqueduct was probably built by Herod the Great to bring water from the Carmel range to Caesarea, the Roman capital of Palestine. Remarkably intact, the aqueduct bears the inscriptions of the Sixth and Tenth Roman Legions, which served in Palestine under the Emperor Hadrian.

III. THE HISTORIC PAST:
The Common Era

From the transitional years — those connecting "B.C.E." with "C.E." — and the first century to the twentieth century is a long and eventful period. What has happened in Palestine during this time?

A. PERIOD OF TRANSITION:
THE ROMAN PERIOD (63 B.C.E.-379 C.E.)

The Roman period, inaugurated by the taking of Jerusalem by Pompey in 63 B.C.E. and marked by the city's destruction by Titus in 70 C.E., lasted until 379 C.E.

According to the usually accepted dating, the Romans appointed Herod "the Great" as king of the Jews in 40 B.C.E.; he took control of Jerusalem three years later (in 37) and reigned until his death in the spring of 4 B.C.E. (though recent study suggests that Herod may have died in the spring of 1 B.C.E.). He was a very great builder: the remains of his works at Jerusalem, Caesarea, Samaria/Sebaste, Masada, and elsewhere are still very impressive. Three of Herod's sons succeeded to as many parts of his kingdom, but one major part — consisting of Judea, Samaria, and Idumea — ruled by Archelaus was soon taken from him and put directly under the rule of Roman governors, who had the titles of prefect and procurator. Only Herod's grandson, Herod Agrippa I (41-44 C.E.), ruled the entire land as king, and gave encouragement to the Jewish religious authorities.

The First Century

The First Revolt. Although rule under Herod's grandson was bearable, the government by the procurators grew increasingly burdensome and objectionable, and led to the Jewish War, also called the First Revolt. This uprising climaxed with the destruction of Jerusalem by the Roman general Titus in 70 C.E. and ended with the taking of Masada by the Roman general Silva in 73.

The theater, a favorite Roman institution, was introduced in Palestine by Herod the Great. This particular theater (now restored) was located at the southern side of Caesarea, facing the sea. It was here that Herod Agrippa became fatally ill.

This intricate mosaic pattern decorates the floor in the western palace of Herod the Great. Herod built this palace and others — as well as powerful fortifications — on the summit and northern terraces of the formidable rock at Masada. Here the First Jewish Revolt against the Romans failed tragically.

In their siege at Masada the Romans built a siege wall — known as the Wall of Circumvallation — that completely encompassed the rock. Armies guarded the periphery of the wall; on its northwest side was the rectangular camp of Silva, the commanding officer.

Built against the northwestern section of the summit wall, facing toward Jerusalem, the synagogue at Masada measures 14x11 m (45x36 ft). It was probably a synagogue already in the Herodian period; certainly it was used as a house of prayer during the Revolt.

Not all of the Jewish leaders supported the First Revolt. One who advised maintaining peace was Yohanan ben Zakkai, a recognized leader of the Pharisaic scribes. During the siege of Jerusalem he made a clever escape: he managed to be carried out of the city in a coffin, and thus reached the Roman camp. From the Romans he received permission to establish a new Jewish center at Yabneh in the coastal plain. There he founded an Academy and gathered a reconstituted Sanhedrin, of which he for a time assumed the presidency (a position which had been held by the high priest while the Temple was standing).

The Historian Josephus. The Jewish historian of the time is Flavius Josephus, who lived from approximately 37 to 95 C.E. His book *Jewish Antiquities* relates the long history of the Jews, and his book *Jewish War* recounts the events of the great war, including the tragic story of the suicide at Masada of the Zealot leader Eleazar ben Yair and his companions, who chose to die rather than fall into the hands of the Romans. Josephus also provides information about the major sects in Judaism at the time: the Pharisees, the Sadducees, the Essenes, and the Zealots, known as "the fourth philosophy."

The theater at Caesarea was modified several times, and in one reconstruction a stone with an inscription of Pontius Pilate's name was reused as an ordinary building stone.

A large-scale outdoor model of Jerusalem graces the grounds of the Holyland Hotel. Made under careful archeological supervision, it recreates the city as it was in the time of the second Temple (prior to the city's destruction in 70 C.E.).

In addition, Josephus is a chief source of information about the Temple as Herod the Great reconstructed it, and about the other structures built under his direction, as well as the three walls of Jerusalem. Today, in the garden of the Holyland Hotel at Jerusalem, there is a large-scale outdoor model of these walls and the city they protected at the time of the second Temple. Designed under the supervision of Michael Avi-Yonah, the model faithfully recreates the structural details mentioned in Josephus' account and suggested by archeological findings.

Early Christianity. It was under Herod the Great that Jesus was born at Bethlehem (Matt. 2:1), and under the procurator Pontius Pilate that he was crucified (Matt. 27:26 and parallel verses). His followers formed the nucleus of the Christian Church, which developed in two ways: under the leadership of James the Just and others, it developed in Palestine as Judaeo-Christianity; guided by the inspiration of Peter (who baptized a Roman centurion), Paul, and others, it developed both in Palestine and in the world beyond as Gentile Christianity. In Palestine, archeologists are finding evidence of the existence of the early Christian community: they have discovered, for example, a private dwelling at Capernaum, believed to have been Peter's home, which was apparently modified to serve as a house-church.

Additional Reading on the Period of the Second Temple and the First Revolt

Grant, Michael. *Herod the Great.* New York: American Heritage Press, 1971. A recent biography, with illustrations.

―――. *The Jews in the Roman World.* New York: Scribner's, 1973. Describes the Herods, Pontius Pilate, and the First and Second Revolts.

―――. *The Twelve Caesars.* New York: Scribner's, 1975. A study that includes a description of the life of Titus, the conqueror of Jerusalem.

Israel, Gérard, and Jacques Lebar. *When Jerusalem Burned.* London: Vallentine, Mitchell, 1973. A vivid story of the great war, including the taking of Jerusalem and the fall of Masada.

McCullough, W. Stewart. *The History and Literature of the Palestinian Jews from Cyrus to Herod, 550 BC to 4 BC.* Toronto: University of Toronto Press, 1975. A study of writings and occurrences from the post-exilic period to the period of the Dead Sea Scrolls and the completion of the canon of the Hebrew Scriptures.

Martin, Ernest L. *The Birth of Christ Recalculated.* 2nd ed. Pasadena and Newcastle, 1980. A publication of the Foundation for Biblical Research, P.O. Box 928, Pasadena, CA 91102.

Perowne, Stewart. *The Later Herods.* London: Hodder and Stoughton, 1958. Describes Herod Antipas, who ruled Galilee in the time of Jesus, Herod Agrippa I, and others.

―――. *The Life and Times of Herod the Great.* London: Hodder and Stoughton, 1957. A careful account of its subject.

Williamson, G. A. *The World of Josephus.* London: Secker and Warburg, 1964. Examines the life and writings of the Jewish historian, and his relationship to the events of his time, particularly the great war.

Yadin, Yigael. *Masada.* London: Weidenfeld and Nicolson, 1966. Details the excavation of Masada, and recounts the events that occurred there.

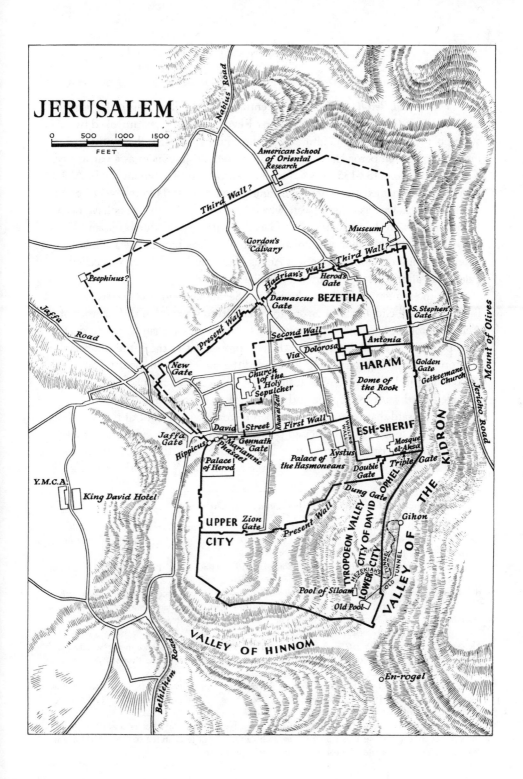

JERUSALEM

0   500   1000   1500
FEET

Nablus Road

Jaffa Road

Third Wall?

American School
of Oriental
Research

Gordon's
Calvary

Museum

Third Wall?

Psephinus?

Hadrian's Wall

Herod's
Gate

Damascus
Gate

BEZETHA

S. Stephen's
Gate

Present Wall

Second Wall

New
Gate

Via Dolorosa

Antonia

HARAM

Mount of Olives

Church
of the
Holy
Sepulcher

Dome of
the Rock

Golden
Gate

Gethsemane
Church

Khan al-Zeit

First Wall

ESH-SHERIF

Jericho Road

David   Street

Jaffa
Gate

Hippicus

Mariamne
Phasael

Gennath
Gate

Palace of
the Hasmoneans

Xystus

Mosque
el-Aksa

WALL

Palace
of Herod

Double
Gate

Triple Gate

Y.M.C.A.

King David Hotel

Dung Gate

OPHEL

Gihon

UPPER

Zion
Gate

Present Wall

TYROPOEON VALLEY

CITY OF DAVID

VALLEY OF THE KIDRON

CITY

LOWER CITY

HEZEKIAH'S

OLD TUNNEL

OLD TUNNEL

Pool of Siloam

Old Pool

VALLEY OF HINNOM

Bethlehem Road

En-rogel

Second Century

The Second Revolt. In the second century C.E. the Jews staged the Second Revolt against the Romans. Like the First Revolt, this one was provoked by attempts to impose foreign culture upon the country, in particular by the intention of the emperor Hadrian (117-138) to rebuild Jerusalem as a pagan city. The Jewish revolt (132-135) was led by Simeon ben Kosiba, whom Rabbi Akiba supported and named Bar-Kokhba, meaning "son of a star" (Num. 24:17). Some of his letters as well as other objects which belonged to his followers have been found in caves on the west side of the Dead Sea (the Wadi Murabbaat and Nahal Hever). After the rebellion was crushed, Jerusalem was named Aelia Capitolina (after the emperor, whose name was Aelius Hadrianus), and Judea was called Palaestina, after the long-departed Philistines.

At the request of Hadrian, the Roman Senate decreed "that it was forbidden to all circumcised persons to enter and to stay within the territory of Aelia Capitolina; any person contravening this prohibition shall be put to death." This prohibition applied not just to the city proper but to the entire municipal territory of Aelia Capitolina, which included the mountains immediately surrounding it, known as Oreine (called "the hill country" in Luke 1:65), and extended northward to Gophna and southward to Herodium and Bethlehem; hence it was said that Jews were forbidden to come within sight of the city. Since the decree excluded "all circumcised persons" from the territory, it also applied to the Judaeo-Christian community. As a consequence of the decree, from the time of Hadrian onward there were Gentile rather than Jewish bishops of the

---

Additional Reading on the Bible, Jesus, and Early Christianity

Bagatti, B. *The Church from the Circumcision,* and *The Church from the Gentiles in Palestine.* Jerusalem: Franciscan Printing Press, 1971. The two branches of early Christianity in Palestine are discussed in the light of recent research.

Blinzler, Joseph. *The Trial of Jesus.* Cork, Ireland: Mercier Press, 1959. A balanced account.

Daniélou, Jean. *Primitive Christian Symbols.* Baltimore: Helicon Press, 1964. Traces the development of many early Christian symbols, such as the Taw cross, that are Jewish in origin.

Goldstein, Morris. *Jesus in the Jewish Tradition.* New York: Macmillan, 1950. Details the references to Jesus of Nazareth in the Rabbinic and Talmudic sources.

Lessing, Erich. *The Bible: A Pictorial Narration,* and *Jesus: A Pictorial Narration.* New York: Herder and Herder, 1970, 1971. Two books with pictures of landscapes and sites associated with Biblical history and the life of Jesus, and of objects of art and culture from the Bronze Age to Roman times.

Mancini, Ignazio. *Archaeological Discoveries Relative to the Judaeo-Christians.* Jerusalem: Franciscan Printing Press, 1970. A brief account of discoveries at Talpiot, Dominus flevit, Bethphage, Nazareth, Capernaum, and other sites.

Toynbee, Arnold, ed. *The Crucible of Christianity.* New York: World Publishing, 1969. Includes the work of contributors such as David Flusser, who writes about Jesus in the context of history, and Jean Daniélou, who defines the early Christians as a Jewish sect.

church in Jerusalem, as we are explicitly told by Eusebius (*Church History* IV, 5-6).

The Dispersion. The Greek word *Diaspora,* rendered as *Dispersion* in English, literally means "a scattering," and is used to refer to the existence of the Jewish people in all lands outside their homeland. In part this scattering was involuntary, due to exile: in the eighth century B.C.E., for example, the people were exiled to Assyria, and in the sixth century B.C.E., to Babylonia; and other deportations took place in other wars.

But scattering was also the result of voluntary choice; in fact, in some interpretations the term *Dispersion* is understood to refer properly to the voluntary residence of Jews in lands other than their homeland. Actually, Jews began living abroad voluntarily already when Cyrus II took Babylon: in his first year of rule there (538/537) he decreed that the exiles might return home, but some of the Jews in Babylonia chose to remain rather than go back to Jerusalem. Another example — from the fifth century B.C.E. — is provided by the existence of a military colony of Jews at Elephantine in Upper Egypt, a group mentioned in the Elephantine Papyri. In the first and second centuries C.E. the process of scattering was much accelerated when many Jews left Palestine by choice in the days of the Jewish War and the Bar-Kokhba rebellion against the Romans, and during the bitter persecution which Hadrian unleashed against the Jews after the Second Revolt. In the time of the Roman empire it is estimated that there were three to four million Jews in the Dispersion from Asia Minor to Spain, constituting seven to eight percent of the total population of the empire, and one million Jews in Palestine proper.

Eventually Jews were found in almost all lands, both in the East and in the West — in Arabia, India, China, Africa, Europe, the Americas, Australia, New Zealand, and elsewhere. Although the homeland was left behind, and its Temple long since destroyed, everywhere in the Dispersion the essential character of Judaism was maintained, largely through the two institutions which could be established wherever there was a community of Jews — namely, the synagogue and the Academy, which were the direct continuation of the synagogues and

---

Additional Reading about Hadrian, Bar-Kokhba, and the Second Revolt

Harris, J. Rendel. "Hadrian's Decree of Expulsion of the Jews from Jerusalem." *HTR,* 19 (1926), 199-206.

Perowne, Stewart. *Hadrian.* London: Hodder and Stoughton, 1960. Details the life of the emperor, and presents a critical view of the Jewish revolt as hopeless.

Yadin, Yigael. *Bar-Kokhba.* New York: Random House, 1971. A first-hand account of the exploration of the almost inaccessible caves of Bar-Kokhba and his followers, and the finding of the materials from the time of the Second Revolt. Illustrated.

academies of Palestine and Babylonia. Both institutions stressed education; the Academy in particular became a place of secular as well as of Talmudic study. Clearly an educated people, the Jews — in many lands where they lived — made notable contributions in almost every field, from literature to politics, from music to science, and from industry to finance. Yet in many lands they suffered suppression, persecution, expulsion — even death.

Jews of the Dispersion today have varying opinions about how they should live in foreign lands: some think that being assimilated by the surrounding culture is desirable, whereas others believe it is essential to maintain Jewish identity and culture. Among the latter group, some believe that it is possible to remain truly Jewish outside of Israel; others do not, and are completely committed to the ideal of a Jewish homeland.

In Tel Aviv there is now a Museum of the Jewish Diaspora called Beth Hatefutsoth, which has exhibits highlighting the life and contributions of the Jews of the Dispersion from 70 C.E. onward. As a text on one wall puts it, what is shown is "a continuous drama of settlement and expulsion, disaster and recovery."

Jews in Palestine. In spite of the widespread scattering in many lands, some Jews always remained in Palestine. It has been noted above that, in spite of the fall of Jerusalem and the destruction of the Temple in 70 C.E., Yohanan ben Zakkai was able thereafter to establish a new spiritual center at Yabneh, with an Academy and a reconstituted Sanhedrin, of which he served for a time as the president. After the Bar-Kokhba revolt, this center was moved to Lower Galilee — first to Usha, then to Beth Shearim, later to Sepphoris, and finally to Tiberias — because more Jews were then to be found in the north than in the south in Judea.

Religious leadership underwent some interesting and important changes. In 85 C.E. the aged Yohanan ben Zakkai was succeeded at Yabneh by Rabban

---

Additional Reading on the Dispersion

Keller, Werner. *Diaspora: The Post-Biblical History of the Jews.* New York: Harcourt, Brace and World, 1969. An account that includes events of the recent past, and details various persecutions as well as Jewish contributions to society.

Poliakov, Léon. *From the Time of Christ to the Court Jews.* Vol. I of *The History of Anti-Semitism.* New York: Vanguard Press, 1965. This volume traces anti-Semitism from pagan antiquity; Poliakov intends to write an additional three volumes to finish the sad story, which will include an exploration of anti-Semitism in modern times. See Vol. I, p. 5 in this work for the estimated number of Jews in the Roman empire and in Palestine, as cited in the paragraph above.

Wernick, Robert. "At Last There Is a Visual Account of the Wanderings of the Jews," with photographs by Dmitri Kessel. *Smithsonian,* 9, No. 3 (June 1978), 32-43. (This magazine is published by Smithsonian Associates, 900 Jefferson Dr., Washington, D.C. 20560.)

Gamaliel II. The latter was one of a line of rabbis who claimed descent from the house of the famous teacher Hillel, who in turn claimed descent from the house of David. Of these descendants of Hillel, no less than six bore the name of Gamaliel. Gamaliel I the Elder, a grandson of Hillel who is mentioned in the Book of Acts (in Acts 5:34-39; 22:3), was the first to have the title Rabban (meaning "our master"), considered a higher title than Rabbi (meaning "my master"). Rabban Gamaliel II, the grandson of Gamaliel I, succeeded him, and the grandson of Gamaliel II ultimately succeeded him; this pattern finally ended only because Gamaliel VI, who died in 425, had no son. In their headship of the Sanhedrin, these men — from Rabban Gamaliel II onward — were given the titles of patriarch and nasi (prince), and were recognized by the Romans as the official representatives of the Jewish nation both in Palestine and in the Dispersion. In Palestine itself they exercised the powers of legislator, judge, and administrator. Only after the death of Gamaliel VI did the Emperor Theodosius II, in 429, declare that the patriarchate was at an end.

Although Jerusalem was not forgotten, Hadrian's interdict of Jewish presence in the entire territory of Aelia Capitolina shifted the center of Jewish

Christian pilgrims began coming to Palestine at least as early as the second century, and the Church of the Holy Sepulcher, built under Constantine, was naturally one of the places they most wanted to visit. This engraving in a chapel of the church records the pilgrims' journey.

life to the north. Officially the Roman prohibition remained in force up to the fourth century C.E., when it was relaxed to the extent that Jewish pilgrims were permitted to come to the Temple site once a year on the ninth day of the Jewish month of Ab, which the rabbis reckoned as the date of the destruction of the sanctuary in both 586 B.C.E. and 70 C.E. Later, in the fifth century C.E., the ban was completely canceled, and Jews were again allowed to settle in the city.

Even in earlier centuries, however, the Roman guard around Jerusalem was not always maintained as strictly as it had been when the decree was first issued. There is even some evidence in Talmudic sources that some Jews managed to visit the city — possibly already in the second century, and certainly in the third. For example, in the first half of the third century it is recorded that a donkey driver named Simeon Kamtra asked the rabbis if, during his business travels, he would have to rend his garments every time he passed Jerusalem, a ritual required of those who looked upon the desolation of the Temple. Similarly, in the second half of the same century Rabbi Yohanan, a prominent scholar, contrasted the earthly Jerusalem with the heavenly city by saying, "Anyone who wants to go up there, can go."

In addition, already in the second and early third centuries there is mention for the first time of Christian pilgrims from abroad visiting sacred sites in Palestine; as Gentiles, they were of course free to come to Jerusalem. One of these was Melito, Bishop of Sardis in Asia Minor, who visited the Holy Land in about 160 C.E. Of the sites associated with Christian history, he said, "I went to the East and came to the place where these things were preached and done." Another pilgrim was Alexander, a bishop in Cappadocia, who came to Jerusalem in 212 C.E. "for the purpose of prayer and investigation of the places" (Eusebius, *Church History* IV, 26, 13; VI, 11, 2).

Third Century

The Mishnah. At the end of the second and the beginning of the third century, the Patriarch Judah I ha-Nasi (the Prince) established his residence and the seat of the Sanhedrin first at Beth Shearim and later at Sepphoris. Completed at Sepphoris under his leadership was the great compilation of ancient traditions and customs called the Mishnah (from the Hebrew *shanah,* meaning "to repeat," and referring to instruction by oral law). He died about 220 C.E. and was buried at Beth Shearim, where, during the third and fourth centuries, a very extensive Jewish catacomb was developed.

Many synagogues were also built during this time, particularly in Galilee. Examples of still-impressive synagogue ruins (of synagogues probably built at the end of the second century or in the beginning of the third) can be seen at Capernaum and Chorazim near the Sea of Galilee; at Baram in the mountains of

The beautiful facade of a large synagogue at the abandoned village of Kefar Baram in northern Galilee has been well preserved, its doors and windows practically undamaged. The facade faces south, in the direction of Jerusalem.

Shadows pattern the walls of the basilica hall of the Capernaum synagogue, which is about 20 x 18 m (65 x 60 ft) in size, with a court to the east, 11 m (30 ft) wide at its front. In the interior colonnades surround the central nave on three sides.

Some think the pentagram (shown here in the Capernaum synagogue) and the hexagram (shown in Fig. 25) originally had magical meaning. Later they were considered symbols of Judaism, and were called the Seal of Solomon and the Shield of David, respectively.

Upper Galilee; and at Meron, northwest of Safad. At the end of the third or the beginning of the fourth century (the period indicated by the coins found on the site), a synagogue was built at Caesarea, on the wall of which was a marble plaque listing the twenty-four priestly courses (I Chron. 24:7-19; Neh. 12:1-21) and the towns in Galilee in which these groups were then settled. Only a

In Hitler's Germany, where the swastika was the emblem of the National Socialist Party, the six-pointed star, made of two equilateral triangles, was the commonly used symbol for Judaism. This representation in stone is found in the Capernaum synagogue.

A major symbol of Judaism is the seven-branched lampstand (menorah) of the Tabernacle (Ex. 25:31) and of the Temple, represented here in the Capernaum synagogue. Flanking it are representations of the ram's horn (shofar), blown to signal festivals (cf. Josh. 6:5), and the shovel, in which incense was burned.

fragment of the inscription is preserved, but it contains the Hebrew names of Nazareth and Migdal (Magdala).

About the year 230 the Christian scholar Origen settled at Caesarea and founded an important school something like the one at Alexandria, of which he had previously been the leader.

Fourth Century

Constantine I the Great and Helena. In the fourth century Constantine I the
Great (sole ruler of the Roman empire, 323-337 C.E.) became a Christian. His
mother Helena came to the Holy Land (only shortly before her death at the age
of eighty in about 327), where she supposedly found the "true cross," and also
founded the Church of the Nativity at Bethlehem, the Church of the Holy
Sepulcher in Jerusalem, and the Eleona Church on the Mount of Olives.
Thereafter many more Christian pilgrims came from abroad: the Bordeaux
Pilgrim (333); Aetheria, who was also called Egeria (385); and others. Eusebius
served as bishop and did his writing at Caesarea (c. 325), and Jerome settled at
Bethlehem and did his writing there (c. 385).

The building of the Constantinian Church of the Holy Sepulcher (known as
the Anastasis) involved the destruction of a shrine of Venus which Hadrian had
put up on this site. With the completion of this and other church buildings,
Jerusalem was transformed from a city with predominantly pagan monuments to
a city with predominantly Christian ones. The ruin of a particular pagan
monument was saved to serve a Christian purpose. At the site of the former
Jewish Temple Hadrian had built a shrine to Jupiter, which featured a statue of
Jupiter and a statue of himself. The Christians doubtless removed these, but
otherwise they left the area in ruins (the state in which it apparently had been
ever since its destruction in 70 C.E.). As Eusebius tells us (in *Theophany*,
Chapter IV), this was done purposefully, in order that the desolation might serve
as a demonstration that Jesus' prediction in Matthew 23:38 had come true:
"Behold, your house is forsaken and desolate."

The Revolt against Gallus. It was Constantine who altered the old edict of
exclusion and officially allowed the Jews to go up to Jerusalem on the ninth day
of Ab to lament the destroyed Temple. In general he enforced the laws of the
empire with impartiality as far as the Jews were concerned, but in
communications to church leaders he was hostile. His oldest son, Constantius II,
became ruler of the entire empire in 350, and in the next year appointed his
nephew Gallus to rule the East as vice-emperor, or caesar.

Constantius II issued new edicts restricting the Jews, and verbally defamed
them; consequently, in 351, encouraged by a war of the Persian king Shapur II
against the Romans, the Jews revolted against Gallus Caesar. Eusebius records in
the *Chronicle* (revised by Jerome) that the Jews slaughtered an entire Roman
garrison in the night and afterward declared open rebellion, to which Gallus
responded by killing thousands of people, even infants. He also destroyed what
were evidently the chief centers of revolt — the towns of Diocaesarea (another
name for Sepphoris), Tiberias, and Lydda — and set fire to many other towns as
well.

The Church of the Nativity at Bethlehem was built under Constantine, and rebuilt in what is basically its present form by Justinian (527-565 C.E.). Under the floor of the present church are sections of the highly intricate floor mosaic of the Constantinian church. A meticulous geometric pattern is shown here.

Julian. Gallus was deposed and executed in 354 C.E., and Constantius II died in 361, whereupon Gallus' younger brother, Julian, became master of the Roman empire (361-363). Called "the Apostate" by the Christians, Julian was an adherent of the Old Hellenic religion and the Neo-Platonic philosophy. He strove to revive pagan religion by reopening the temples and restoring the cults of the old gods; at the same time he attempted to minimize the influence of the Christians in the empire, who by this time constituted thirty to forty percent of the population.

Partly to use the Jews as a counterbalance to the Christians and partly to gain their support for a war he projected with Persia, he favored them. In particular, as he traveled to the East, he met a delegation of Jews in Antioch and ordered both that Jerusalem and the surrounding area should be restored to them and that the Temple should be rebuilt. In fact, a stone has been found in the Western Wall of the Temple area in Jerusalem with a Hebrew inscription which quotes Isaiah 66:14: "You shall see, and your heart shall rejoice; your bones shall flourish like the grass." The inscription, probably made in this time period, is almost certainly an expression of the joy with which Julian's decree was received. On his Persian campaign, however, Julian lost his life, and the project came to an end.

It was not long after Julian's reign that the old laws were in effect again, and, as before, the Jews were allowed to come to Jerusalem only on the ninth day of Ab to lament the destruction of the Temple. Jerome (in his *Commentary on Zephaniah* 1:15) notes that they even had to buy permits to mourn, and he describes (but apparently without sympathy) the pitiful spectacle of the old men and old women, the infirm and the weak — all dressed in rags — as they came on the anniversary day.

Elsewhere in the land, however, synagogues were being built or rebuilt. The ruins of the synagogue at Hamath (near Tiberias) provide an especially fine example of decorative mosaic flooring from the fourth century. Depicted are the signs of the zodiac and the symbols of the seasons.

Just as more synagogues were being built, so many more churches were being built, because the Christian population of the land was increasing. When Eusebius wrote his *Onomasticon* in about 330, he mentioned only three Christian towns; when Jerome revised the work in Latin in 390, he added to the descriptions of many locations the names of churches which had by then been built there.

B. BYZANTINE PERIOD (379-640 C.E.)

In 330 C.E. the emperor Constantine I inaugurated a new capital at the former Greek city of Byzantium on the Bosporus, calling it New Rome and Constantinople; thus the Byzantine period is sometimes said to have begun in the year 330. It was only during the reign of Theodosius I the Great (379-395), however, that the empire was divided permanently into the East and the West, Palestine naturally falling under the rule of the Byzantine emperors. From this historical viewpoint the Byzantine period may thus be considered to begin in 379 C.E.

Fifth Century

Theodosius I was succeeded by his two sons, Honorius (395-423) in the West and Arcadius (395-408) in the East. Already during the reign of Honorius Rome was sacked by barbarian invaders (410), and the emperor withdrew to Ravenna; by 476 Odoacer was the first barbarian ruler of Italy, and the Roman empire in the West came to an end. In the East, Arcadius was succeeded by his son

Theodosius II (408-450), who in turn was succeeded by a long line of rulers. In fact, Roman rule was maintained there until Constantinople fell to the Crusaders in 1204 and became the seat of a Latin empire, then was recaptured for the Byzantines by Michael VIII Palaeologus in 1261.

Theodosius II. Under the Byzantine rulers, who were orthodox Christians, the leaders of the church found increased opportunity to obtain imperial actions against both Hellenism and Judaism. Thus from the fifth century onward Hellenism virtually disappeared as a factor of historical importance; Judaism did not disappear, but suffered severe restrictions. When the Patriarch Gamaliel VI died (in 425), Theodosius II did not confirm a successor (although presumably there were still members of the House of Hillel who could have succeeded Gamaliel), and in a law of 429 the emperor noted the "end of the patriarchs."

In a related attempt to weaken the Jews, the emperor tried to divide them in various ways. He first divided Palestine into three provinces — Palaestina Prima (Judea, Samaria, the coastal plain, and Perea east of the Jordan); Palaestina Secunda (Galilee and the Hellenistic cities of the Decapolis); and Palaestina Tertia (the Negev and Arabia Petrea, with Petra as its capital). These remained the administrative divisions until the Muslim conquest. The emperor also established two Sanhedrins: in addition to the one at Tiberias (in Palaestina Secunda), he established another at Caesarea (in Palaestina Prima). Nevertheless, the Jews remained primarily loyal to the Sanhedrin at Tiberias.

In other laws, the majority of which were established in 438, the Jews were forbidden to hold public office, to build new synagogues, and to convert Christians to Judaism.

Eudocia. In 421 Theodosius II took as empress a Hellene named Athenais, whose father was a teacher of Greek at the University of Athens. She became a Christian and changed her name to Eudocia. Becoming estranged from Theodosius, Eudocia visited Jerusalem in 439, and in 443 went back to live there permanently until her death in about 460. She was responsible for extending the city wall on the south, so that it again enclosed Mount Zion on the west and Ophel on the east, as it had in earlier times; and through her influence the Jews were also once again allowed to visit the city more freely, and probably allowed to settle there, too.

There are remains of a number of fine Palestinian synagogues built in the fifth century, the number suggesting that, even after there was a ban on such construction, the prohibition may not have been enforced consistently. Many of these structures are impressive in design. At Isifiya on Mount Carmel, for example, a synagogue built in approximately the second half of the fifth century has a decorative mosaic floor showing a seven-branched lampstand, a ram's horn,

This beautiful floor mosaic graces the Benedictine Church of the Multiplication of the Loaves and Fishes (at Tabgha), built to mark the supposed site of the feeding of the multitude. This particular design depicts birds — the heron, dove, and cormorant — and plants — the lotus and oleander — common to the region.

plants used in Jewish ritual, and a wreath of flowers surrounding a Hebrew inscription, which reads, "Shalom el Yisrael" ("Peace be to Israel").

The Palestinian Talmud. The rabbis naturally continued their scholarly work, and at Tiberias during the fifth century they added the commentary known as the Gemara (meaning "completion") to the text of the Mishnah to create the complete Palestinian Talmud (meaning "instruction"), the great body of Jewish civil and canonical law.

Before the end of the fifth century Christians constituted the majority of the population in the land, and continued to build more churches. Examples of their productivity abound. There is a small chapel, for example, at Tabgha, on

Also found in the Benedictine Church is this floor mosaic. Located behind the altar, it is a primitive but striking representation (probably made in the fourth century) of a basket of cross-marked loaves set between two fish, commemorating the miracle of the loaves and fishes.

the shore of the Sea of Galilee, supposedly the place where Jesus multiplied the loaves and fishes. Probably built in the fourth century, it was replaced at the end of the fourth or the beginning of the fifth century by a larger basilica, which has a decorative mosaic floor depicting the fauna and flora near the lake. At Jerusalem, outside the north gate, Eudocia built a splendid church over what is probably the place where Stephen was stoned and buried. At Nazareth, a fifth-century basilica was erected over what had apparently been an earlier house-church, believed to be the house of Mary, Jesus' mother. In the year 484 the Samaritans revolted against the emperor Zeno (474-491); after he suppressed the revolt, he built a Christian church on Mount Gerizim at the site where the Samaritan temple had once stood.

The handsome, modern Franciscan Basilica of the Annunciation at Nazareth commemorates the supposed site of the home of Mary, Jesus' mother. Presumably, this is the place to which the pilgrim known as the Anonymous of Piacenza (570 C.E.) refers when he notes, "The house of St. Mary is a basilica."

Excavations conducted during the building of the modern church of the Annunciation have revealed the remains of a church probably dating from before the time of Constantine. Built like a synagogue, it is marked with graffiti and symbols probably inscribed by Jewish Christians.

Sixth Century

By the sixth century the Jews had declined to a relatively small minority in Palestine, estimated at 150,000 to 200,000 persons, or ten to fifteen percent of the total population. Nevertheless, they built some fine synagogues during this century, notably the one at Beth Alpha at the foot of Mount Gilboa in the Valley of Jezreel. Marked with a date that occurred during the reign of the emperor Justin — probably Justin I (518-527) — the mosaic floor in this synagogue depicts the signs of the zodiac, Abraham's intended sacrifice of Isaac, and the Ark of the Law.

Tiberias was still the seat of the Sanhedrin and of the Academy (Yeshivah), the chief school of rabbinic studies, and thus remained the spiritual and intellectual center of Jewish life. About 520 Mar Zutra, son of the head of the Jews in Babylonia, arrived at Tiberias and soon became head of the Sanhedrin. He was succeeded by his descendants for seven generations, until the school was moved from Tiberias to Jerusalem in the middle of the eighth century.

The Babylonian Talmud. In Babylonia there were also important academies, the two principal ones being at Sura and at Nehardea (where there was an ancient synagogue believed to have been built by King Jehoiachin). During the sixth century scholars in these two academies completed the Babylonian Talmud, which eventually surpassed even the Palestinian Talmud in importance. Through these works the beliefs and practices of Judaism were further defined and developed.

Justinian I the Great. After the Council of Chalcedon (held in 451), the Christian church was divided between the Orthodox (who accepted the Chalcedonian belief that Christ had two separate natures, human and divine) and the Monophysites (who believed in "one nature" that was both human and divine). As emperor, Justinian I the Great (527-565) undertook to repress all "heretics," a term he re-defined to include not only Christians who disagreed with the established church (therefore the Monophysites in particular), but also all who were not orthodox (which included the Jews and Samaritans).

Accordingly, Justinian reaffirmed old laws and issued new regulations, which restricted Jews and Samaritans. An example is the stipulation that the Jews might not keep the Passover at its proper date if that date fell before the Christian Easter. But the most drastic change was the suspension of the old law, which before had at least given Judaism the legal status of a permitted and lawful religion (*religio licita*), a benefit which the Samaritans had never enjoyed. Under these new pressures the Samaritans revolted again in 529, 556, and 578, the first two of these uprisings occurring under Justinian I, and the last under his successor, Justin II (565-578). In 556 and 578 Jews joined with Samaritans in insurrection, but the rebels were both times crushed by the superior forces of the Byzantines.

A persecutor of the Jews, Justinian I favored the Christians: he was a great builder of Christian churches. In addition to his works at Constantinople, Ephesus, and elsewhere, in Palestine he rebuilt the Constantinian Church of the Nativity at Bethlehem; the present church, in fact, is still essentially his structure. The pilgrim Theodosius, who came to Palestine in 530, noted in his itinerary details about the holy places as they were known at that time. In addition, the so-called Anonymous of Piacenza (earlier called Antoninus Martyr), who came in 570, described the sanctuaries as they were at the height of the Byzantine period. When he visited Nazareth, for example, he noted, "The house of St. Mary is a basilica." The Madaba Mosaic Map provides similar information. Made about 560 as the mosaic floor of a church at this site in Transjordan, it corresponds at many points with the *Onomasticon* of Eusebius. It is quite well-preserved, and shows many sites and churches; fortunately, its representation of Jerusalem as it was at this time is almost completely intact.

Seventh Century

The pressure upon Judaism was intensified still more at the beginning of the seventh century when the Byzantine emperor Phocas (602-610) attempted to force the Jews of the entire empire, including Palestine, to accept Christianity and be baptized. Soon, however, came the Persian invasion.

The Persian Invasion. Now ruled by the Sassanian dynasty (229-651 C.E.), Persia had been struggling against the Roman and Byzantine empires throughout most of its history. At this point, under Chosroes II (590-628), the Persians made their most successful thrust westward. In 611 they captured Antioch; in 613 they took Damascus, and then advanced upon Palestine. Here the Jews, who had suffered so much under Byzantine rule, welcomed the invaders and assisted them with a force of 20,000 or more Jewish soldiers. Caesarea, the capital, was taken, and then Jerusalem, in 614, after a siege of only twenty days. Throughout the land the churches were destroyed, including the Eleona Church on the Mount of Olives and the Church of the Holy Sepulcher in Jerusalem, where the "true cross" was among the treasures taken away. Only the Church of the Nativity at Bethlehem was spared, because the invaders saw on it a mosaic of the adoration of the Magi in which the Magi were clothed in Persian dress.

Heraclius. The Jews were now left in control of Jerusalem, but only for three years (from 614 to 617), after which the Persians evidently thought it more politic to favor the Christian majority in the land, and returned the city to

Christian control. In any case the Persian occupation of Palestine lasted only fifteen years. In 629 C.E. the Byzantine emperor Heraclius (610-642) recovered the land and also the "true cross." At first Heraclius promised no revenge upon the Jews for their assistance of the Persians, but then under pressure from the Christian priests in Jerusalem broke his word and persecuted them, even expelling them from the city.

Now, however, both the Byzantine and the Persian empires were virtually exhausted by their mutual struggle, and both Orthodox Christians and Persian Zoroastrians had become so intolerant that they had created much dissatisfaction in their respective areas. A new and more freshly vigorous force was about to take advantage of these circumstances, initiating a change of masters that was going to be regarded hopefully by many Jews.

Muhammad and the Orthodox Caliphs. In 622 C.E., while the Persians occupied Palestine, the Arabian prophet Muhammad emigrated from Mecca to Medina (a pilgrimage called the Hegira, from which the first year of the Muslim era is reckoned); in 629, when Heraclius was regaining the Holy Land, Muhammad was completing his conquest of Mecca. In 632 the prophet died, and was followed by a succession of four so-called Orthodox caliphs (successors) — Abu Bakr (632-634), Umar (634-644), Uthman (644-656), and Ali (656-661). Under their rule Syria, Palestine, Iraq, Persia, and Egypt were all subjugated to Islam.

In 636 the Arab army defeated the Byzantine army at the Yarmuk River, and the Byzantines evacuated Palestine. In 638 Jerusalem surrendered; in 640 Caesarea, the last Byzantine stronghold, was taken after a seven-month siege. Thus Byzantine Palestine was no more; the Arab period had begun.

C. ARAB PERIOD (640-1099 C.E.)

The primary motive of the Arab conquest was evidently economic: what the new conquerors chiefly expected of the new subjects was the payment of tribute rather than conversion to Islam. In Arabia Muhammad had slaughtered some

---

Additional Reading on the Period from the Second Century C.E. to the Arab Conquest

Avi-Yonah, M. *The Jews of Palestine: A Political History from the Bar Kokhba War to the Arab Conquest.* New York: Schocken Books, 1976. Explains how the Roman and Byzantine rulers handled Palestine, and explores the relationship of Byzantine Christianity to Judaism.

Shanks, Hershel. *Judaism in Stone: The Archaeology of Ancient Synagogues.* New York: Harper & Row; Washington, D.C.: Biblical Archaeology Society, 1979. The story of ancient Jewish synagogues from before the destruction of Jerusalem in 70 C.E. to the Arab conquest, told on the basis of archeological discovery. Especially important is its discussion of the debate over the date of the famous synagogue at Capernaum, which gives reasons for fixing the date at the end of the second or the beginning of the third century.

Jews who had refused to accept his leadership, and had exiled others; still others he had decided to protect because they had paid land and poll taxes, this decision setting an important precedent. He also recognized both Jews and Christians as "people of the Book"; especially for this reason both groups were often allowed to live in peace under Muslim protection — providing, of course, that they paid the required taxes.

Umar and Sophronius. When Abu Bakr first led his army out of Arabia, he reportedly said to them: "Be just, for the unjust never prosper. Be valiant: die rather than retreat. Keep your word, even to your enemies. Be merciful: slay neither the old, nor the young, nor the women. Destroy no fruit trees, no crops, no beasts. Kill neither sheep, nor oxen nor camels, except it be for food." Nevertheless, the conquest of Palestine was primarily a military endeavor, and in its course many Jews, Samaritans, and Christians were killed indiscriminately.

At Jerusalem it was the patriarch Sophronius, as the head of the Christian community, who surrendered the city to the caliph Umar without a struggle. As the two discussed the conditions of submission, the patriarch expressed his wish that no Jews be allowed to settle in the city, but the caliph, in recognition of Jewish help in the Muslim conquest of the land, asked that 200 families be accepted as inhabitants. In the end they agreed that 70 families from Tiberias be allowed to settle in the southern part of Jerusalem. A document discovered in the nineteenth century in the Cairo Genizah (meaning "hiding place," the name for a synagogue storeroom) records this agreement.

According to the Arab Christian writer Eutychius of Alexandria (940 C.E.), Umar visited the Church of the Holy Sepulcher with Sophronius and gave the patriarch a charter guaranteeing that the church would not be taken over for Muslim prayers. The two also visited the Temple area, Eutychius tells us, and Umar himself cleared away the filth accumulated on the Sacred Rock in the center.

According to Jewish tradition this Sacred Rock was the one upon which Abraham almost sacrificed Isaac, as well as the marker of the site of David's altar and the altar of Solomon's Temple. According to Muslim tradition the rock was the one from which Muhammad ascended to heaven during his famous Night Journey. The text in the Koran (Surah XVII, 1) reads: "Glorified be He who carried His servant by night from the Sacred Mosque to the Farthest Mosque . . . that We might show him of Our tokens." This was interpreted and amplified to mean that Muhammad, accompanied by the angel Gabriel and mounted on a white horse named Buraq ("lightning"), rode through the sky from the Kaabah at Mecca to the Sacred Rock in Jerusalem, and from there was caught up through the seven heavens into the presence of Allah.

To commemorate this event, Umar built a mosque in the Temple area, probably at the south end where the often-rebuilt Mosque al-Aqsa (Farthest Mosque) still stands. Arculf (670), the first Christian pilgrim of record in the Holy Land after the Arab conquest, describes the building: "In that renowned place where once the temple had been magnificently constructed...the Saracens [as the Christians called the Muslims] now frequent a quadrangular house of prayer, which they have built rudely, constructing it by raising planks and great beams on some remains of ruins." He adds that it reportedly could hold three thousand worshipers.

Although Palestine was now under Arab control, the process by which the land became predominantly Arabic and Islamic was slow; in fact, several centuries passed before the majority of the population came to speak the Arabic language and were converted to the teachings of Muhammad. Contributing to the land's gradual change was the occasional influx of Arab immigrants, especially from Arabia and Egypt. This flow continued — at least intermittently — from the seventh century to the twentieth century.

The Umayyad Dynasty. The next rulers of the Islamic empire were the Arabs of the Umayyad dynasty (661-750 C.E.). They ruled at Damascus, although the founder of the dynasty, Muawiyah, came to Jerusalem to be proclaimed caliph. In 691 the caliph Abd al-Malik (685-705) built over the Sacred Rock in the Temple area the magnificent Dome of the Rock, intended to compete in grandeur with the Christians' Church of the Holy Sepulcher. Thus the two major monuments in Jerusalem were Muslim and Christian.

Despite the dominance of these two groups, some Jews were settled there again. Although excluded from the Temple area, they were allowed to purchase the slope of the Mount of Olives across from the Temple area to use for religious festivals and for a burial ground. Of course, in other parts of the country there were Jewish settlements, too. At Hebron, for example, the Jews were allowed to build a synagogue in front of the entrance to the Cave of Machpelah. And at Tiberias the Academy of the rabbis continued its work, producing during the seventh and eighth centuries the Masoretic system of punctuation for the Hebrew text of the Scriptures and the final Masoretic text of the Hebrew Bible. The period of the Arab conquest and of the rule of the Umayyads, then, was a time of relative peace and productivity for the Jews.

Eighth Century

al-Walid. Under Umayyad rule Jerusalem became a Muslim religious center, surpassed in importance only by Mecca and Medina. The caliph al-Walid (705-715 C.E.), son of Abd al-Malik, replaced the original wooden mosque of

Soon after the surrender of Jerusalem to the Muslim Arabs, the caliph Umar built a mosque in the Temple area. Often rebuilt, this place of prayer is now the al-Aqsa mosque, symbolizing Jerusalem's ranking among the holy cities in the traditions of Islam.

The Dome of the Rock, built by Muslim caliph Abd al-Malik, rises over the great outcropping of natural rock in the center of the Temple area. It is probably the threshing floor of Araunah where David built an altar (II Sam. 24:18), and where the altar of Solomon's temple was placed.

Umar in the Temple area with a more monumental building which, reconstructed several more times since then, still stands as the Mosque al-Aqsa. There were thus two very impressive buildings in the Temple area — this mosque and the Dome of the Rock — which comprised the Haram esh-Sharif, or Noble Sanctuary. Adjacent to it but outside the enclosure walls of the Temple area on the south and southwest an entire complex of large buildings was developed, built over the remains of earlier Byzantine buildings leveled in the process. The chief building was a palace, directly south of the Mosque al-Aqsa. These buildings evidently provided accommodations for numerous residents and probably for many pilgrims from many parts of the Umayyad empire.

Jerusalem was al-Quds (the Holy), the name by which it is known in Arabic even today. Muhammad, quoted by Abu Hurairah (an early recorder of his sayings), declared the importance of this city when he said: "'Among all cities, Allah had singled out four for special esteem, and they are: Mecca — the city of all cities; Medina which is like a palm tree; Jerusalem which compares to an olive tree; and Damascus which is like the fig tree.'"

Suleiman and Ramla. In spite of this regard for Jerusalem, there was only one caliph who chose to make his permanent residence in Palestine. This was the caliph Suleiman (715-717), second son of Abd al-Malik and brother of al-Walid. For his capital Suleiman chose a totally new site, Ramla (8 km or 3 mi southwest of Lod, the ancient Lydda), the name of which means "sand" in Arabic. There he built a palace and a mosque.

Toward the end of the fifth century the Abbasid Caliph Harun al-Rashid built an underground cistern at Ramla, which is still beautifully preserved; at the end of the twelfth century Saladin rebuilt the mosque of Suleiman, a few fragments of which are preserved at the foot of the so-called White Tower. This tower, the most prominent landmark in Ramla, was originally constructed by the Sultan Baibars when he recovered Ramla from the Crusaders in 1268.

Hisham. The caliph Hisham (724-743), the fourth son of Abd al-Malik, also did some building at Ramla, and at Jericho he built for himself a fine winter palace. The latter, however, was destroyed by an earthquake in 747 before it was ever occupied. The ruins are less than 2 km (a little more than 1 mi) north of the Spring of Elisha at Jericho. The finest decoration surviving is the mosaic floor of a small room in a bathhouse complex: it depicts a fruit tree, underneath which a lion is attacking three gazelles. Also interesting to note is that male and female figures were placed alternately in the niches of the entrance porch of the palace, an indication that Islam had not yet adopted the Hebrew prohibition of the portrayal of the human image.

The Abbasid Dynasty. Although the term "Arab Period" is used until the time of the Crusades, the Umayyad dynasty was the only purely Arab dynasty; those who succeeded it were Muslim, but not purely Arab. The next dynasty was that of the Abbasids, who traced their ancestry to an uncle of Muhammad named al-Abbas (though the purity of their ancestry was not maintained). They succeeded the Umayyads in 750 C.E., and in 762 moved their capital from Damascus to Baghdad. They ruled there (and at Samarra from 836 to 892) until Mesopotamia was overrun by the Mongol hordes of Hulagu in 1258. This was the golden age of Islamic civilization, and Baghdad became a city of fabulous wealth and splendor, notably under the caliph Harun al-Rashid (786-809). Unfortunately, from this vantage point Palestine was a relatively remote province, and was generally neglected; it is not surprising, then, that it was often plagued by disorder, involved in various conflicts, and subject to raids by nomadic Bedouins from Transjordan.

In 748 C.E. there was an earthquake in Galilee, and the Academy was moved from Tiberias to Jerusalem. In southern Judea the village of Sussiya provides an example of a Jewish settlement of this time; it has a synagogue with a mosaic floor designed in the eighth or the ninth century.

Ninth Century

Ahmad ibn-Tulun. In 868 C.E. a Turk from east of Samarkand named Ahmad ibn-Tulun (868-884) was sent to Egypt as governor. He made himself independent, and in 877 conquered Palestine and Syria, establishing a fleet and a naval base at Acco (the Hellenistic Ptolemais, also known as Crusader Acre, on the north side of the present Bay of Haifa). From this time on, Egypt rather than Baghdad exerted primary control over Palestine.

Tenth Century

The Fatimids. In the ninth and tenth centuries the Arab population of Palestine grew as the Bedouin tribes entered the land in increasing numbers. In 969 the Fatimid dynasty arose. (They claimed descent from Fatima, the daughter of Muhammad, but this claim was disputed.) They conquered Egypt and went on to take Palestine, ruling until 1091.

In 985 an Arab traveler named Muqaddasi, who was born in Jerusalem, wrote an extended description of Palestine, telling of towns from Tiberias in the north to Gaza and Hebron in the south. He explains that, in the building of the Dome of the Rock at Jerusalem, "they [i.e., the Umayyads] had for a rival and as a comparison the great church [of the Holy Sepulcher] belonging to the Christians...and they built this to be even more magnificent than that other." He describes it as "a marvelous sight to behold, and one such that in all Islam I have never seen its equal; neither have I heard tell of aught built in pagan times that could rival in grace this Dome of the Rock." But he also writes: "Still, Jerusalem has some disadvantages.... Learned men are few, and the Christians numerous, and the same are unmannerly in public places.... The schools are unattended, for there are no lectures. Everywhere the Christians and the Jews have the upper hand, and the mosque is void of either congregation or assembly of learned men."

Eleventh Century

al-Hakim. The Fatimid caliph al-Hakim (996-1021) claimed he was an incarnation of the godhead (a claim accepted by the Druzes, members of an offshoot of Islam still surviving to this day), and launched a persecution of Jews and Christians aimed at converting the "infidels" to Islam. In 1009 he forbade pilgrimages to the Holy Land and ordered the destruction of all synagogues and churches except the Church of the Nativity at Bethlehem. Among others, the Church of the Holy Sepulcher was demolished. To escape al-Hakim's rampage, the scholars of the Academy moved to Ramla and stayed there until 1033, when an earthquake led to abandonment of the town for a time; they returned some time later.

Note: al-Hakim's successors, his son al-Zahir (1021-1035) and grandson al-Mustansir (1035-1094), allowed — in return for various concessions — the rebuilding of the Church of the Holy Sepulcher, which was accomplished with the assistance of the Byzantine emperor Constantine X Monomachus (1042-1054). They also allowed the resumption of pilgrimages.

The Seljuk Turks. Meanwhile, the Seljuk Turks, already converted to Islam, moved westward from their position near the borders of China, overran many lands, and in 1071 drove the Fatimids out of Jerusalem and northern Palestine, only to lose Jerusalem to the Fatimids by 1098. Upon the Seljuk conquest in 1071, the Academy moved to Tyre. Like the Fatimids, the Seljuks persecuted both Jews and Christians, and forbade pilgrimage.

D. CRUSADER PERIOD (1099-1291 C.E.)

The Christian West launched the Crusades largely because of the earlier destruction of the Church of the Holy Sepulcher and because of the interference with pilgrimages by both Fatimids and Seljuks. The conflict between these two

---

Additional Reading on the Arab Period

Hitti, Philip K. *History of the Arabs.* London: Macmillan, 1937. A large, standard, detailed history.

Although remains of the Constantinian church are preserved beneath it, the present Church of the Holy Sepulcher is essentially the same structure that was built by the Crusaders in the twelfth century.

Muslim powers was the primary factor making the Crusaders' entry of the Holy Land relatively easy.

In the summer of 1099 the Crusaders approached Jerusalem, their chief objective. The city, held by a Fatimid garrison of a thousand men, put up a determined resistance, but fell on July 15. All the Muslims and Jews found there — and even some of the native Christians — were massacred. Godfrey de Bouillon, the conqueror, became the head of a new Latin state.

Twelfth Century

Under Godfrey's brother Baldwin (1100-1118), the Kingdom of Jerusalem (Regnum Hierusalem), as it was called, reached its peak of development and power, extending from the Gulf of Alexandretta to the Gulf of Aqabah, and defended by a series of imposing castles.

In Jerusalem the al-Aqsa Mosque became the Temple of Solomon (Templum Salomonis) and the Dome of the Rock became the Temple of the Lord (Templum Domini), re-defined by the cross placed on top of it. A military order of the Crusaders was quartered in the Templum Salomonis and thus called themselves the Knights Templars; another order, after building a hospital south of the Church of the Holy Sepulcher, called themselves the Knights Hospitalers of St. John.

Many churches were rebuilt, including the Church of the Holy Sepulcher — in fact, it is essentially the reconstruction by the Crusaders which stands today. Another Crusader-built church in Jerusalem which still stands, very well-preserved, is the Church of St. Anne, built on what is traditionally considered the site of the home of Joachim and Anne (the parents of Jesus' mother, Mary), and adjacent to the Pool of Bethesda.

In 1169 a prominent Jewish pilgrim arrived in Palestine — Benjamin of Tudela, a Spanish Jew from the town of that name in northern Spain. In the narrative of his travels Benjamin tells of visiting Acre, Haifa, Caesarea, Nablus, Jerusalem, Bethlehem, Hebron, Ashkelon, Tiberias, and Meron, near Safad.

He notes that there were "about two hundred Jewish inhabitants" at Acre. At Nablus he found "Samaritan Jews... who observe the Mosaic Law only," and

Reminders of ancient struggles, this moat and wall were built at Caesarea by the Crusaders, who developed the smallest of the several towns built there. Though the Crusaders took the city from the Muslim Arabs and held it during the twelfth century, the Muslims returned to destroy it in 1291 C.E.

This conically-topped tomb is popularly supposed to be the pillar that Absalom set up for himself in the King's Valley (II Sam. 18:18). Actually, it is one of several tombs in the Kidron Valley from a much later period — probably Hellenistic (dating in the second and first centuries B.C.E.).

who worship "on Mount Gerizim." At Jerusalem he found "a small city fortified with three walls" containing "a numerous population." He lists various Christian sects — Jacobite, Armenian, Greek, and others — and describes the Jewish community as consisting of approximately two hundred persons who dwell "in one corner of the city, under the Tower of David" (i.e., close to the Jaffa Gate, near the present Armenian Quarter). He refers to the Dome of the Rock as the Templum Domini, and says: "In front of it you see the Western Wall, one of the walls which formed the...ancient Temple...and all Jews resort thither to say their prayers near the wall of the courtyard." In the "valley of Jehoshaphat" he saw "the pillar erected on Absalom's place." This Pillar of Absalom is the conically-topped tomb in the Kidron Valley, traditionally considered the burial place of King David's rebel son, but actually a burial monument from a much later time — the second century B.C.E. Benjamin's reference shows that the Valley of Jehoshaphat (Joel 3:2, 12) was identical with the Valley of the Kidron.

Across the Kidron on the slope of the Mount of Olives he noted the ancient Jewish cemetery, observing that "the Christians destroy these monuments, and use the stones in building their houses." On the road to Bethlehem he saw "the monument which points out the grave of Rachel" (Gen. 35:19-20). At Tiberias he found "hot waters which spout forth from under ground" and "warm baths"; he also noted a synagogue in the vicinity. At Meron, near Safad, there was a cave in which were the tombs of Hillel and Shammai, the famed Jewish sages of the first century B.C.E.

Saladin. Counterattack against the Crusaders came relatively soon. Most important in the attempt to drive them out was Saladin (al-Malik al-Nasir Salah ed-Din Yusuf, 1169-1193). He was the founder of the Ayubid dynasty (named for his father, Ayub — or Job — a Kurd and a commander at Baalbek), which supplanted the Fatimid dynasty. Saladin became master of both Egypt and Syria, his kingdom thus surrounding the Latin kingdom on all sides; and in 1187 he decisively defeated Guy de Lusignan, then king of Jerusalem, in battle on the ridge west of Tiberias (known because of its two small peaks as the Horns of Hattin). Soon afterward Jerusalem itself was taken. There the al-Aqsa Mosque was formally handed over to the Muslims again, Christian crosses on the tops of churches were taken down, and the Church of St. Anne was turned into a Muslim college. At the Church of the Holy Sepulcher, however, four Syrian Jacobite priests were permitted to continue services, though the "true cross" was taken away and this time lost forever.

In 1192 a truce between Saladin and Richard the Lion-hearted restored the Kingdom of Jerusalem in name but not in size; and Acco (the Hellenistic Ptolemais) — not Jerusalem — was made the capital of the kingdom. This city the Knights Hospitalers of St. John called St. Jean d'Acre — hence the name "Acre." At Acre is the so-called Crypt of St. John, a magnificent vaulted stone hall under the Turkish Citadel believed to have been the refectory of the knights.

Thirteenth Century

Baibars. Saladin died in 1193, and the Ayubids who followed him were soon opposed by the Mamluks. The latter were white Turkish slaves (*mamluk* means "possessed" or "owned") who became powerful soldiers — so powerful that, in 1250, they ended Ayubid rule in Egypt. The Mamluk Sultan Baibars (1260-1277) carried out a systematic campaign against the cities and castles which remained to the Crusaders, a campaign characterized by ruthless massacres of people and destruction of churches. He took Nazareth, Caesarea, Safad, and Jaffa, and devastated the entire coastal area so that there would be no landing place for his opponents. His successor, al-Ashraf Khalil (1290-1293), made the final conquest of Acre in 1291, and the last of the Crusaders departed in their ships for Cyprus. The Crusaders' kingdom was thus at an end, and the land was in the hands of the Mamluks.

As already noted, Jews had remained in the land throughout the preceding centuries. Although their numbers dwindled, they never disappeared from the land altogether; even during the Crusader period there was a constant trickle of Jewish immigrants coming into the country — some from Europe and some from Islamic territories, especially North Africa. At first the Crusaders forbade Jews to enter Jerusalem, but later relaxed the restrictions and allowed some Jewish settlement there, and also restored visiting rights to Jewish pilgrims from overseas.

A notable visitor among the pilgrims of the thirteenth century was the renowned Jewish scholar from Gerona in Spain, Rabbi Moshe ben Nahman — also known as Nahmanides and as the Ramban — who came in 1267. In a letter of that date to his son in Spain he tells of a massacre of the Jews in Jerusalem seven years before, at which time some had escaped to Shechem (Nablus), carrying with them their Scrolls of the Law. As he also tells in the letter, he was able to convert a ruin, which had marble columns and a dome, into a synagogue; he then had the Torah Scrolls brought back for use there.

Additional Reading on the Crusades

Hitti, Philip K. *Islam and the West.* Princeton: D. Van Nostrand, Anvil Book, 1962. Describes the push of Islam to the West, and the push of the West into the East, especially during the Crusades. Includes selected readings, chiefly from Muslim authors. Dedicated "to those rare souls in Islam and the West who feel at home in both cultures."

Mayer, Hans Eberhard. *The Crusades.* London: Oxford University Press, 1972. Translation of a basic German work. Adequately detailed, with a bibliography and notes which cite a vast supporting literature, including the fundamental sources.

Runciman, Steven. *A History of the Crusades.* 3 vols. New York: Cambridge University Press, 1955-1962. A standard work.

Setton, Kenneth M., editor-in-chief. *A History of the Crusades.* 5 vols. Philadelphia: University of Pennsylvania Press, 1955ff. A very comprehensive work.

In 1473 the synagogue (known as the Ramban synagogue) was forcibly taken from the Jews, then restored to them by the Mamluk sultan. After the Ottoman conquest (1517) it was again appropriated by the Arabs and used as a cheesemaker's shop until recent times, when it once again became a place to worship. Located on the main street of the Jewish Quarter in the Old City, it is probably the oldest synagogue now in use in Jerusalem.

E. MAMLUK PERIOD (1291-1517 C.E.)

By the Mamluk period Palestine had become predominantly a Muslim country, but Jewish settlement was allowed again, too. First of all, much of the land was desolate, because of the many wars that had wracked it, and the many natural calamities that had ravaged it — earthquakes, droughts, famines, epidemics, and plagues of locusts. In addition, because of the extortions of the rulers there was a general collapse of the economy, and Palestine became primarily a land of peasants and of Bedouin. Even for the Muslim populace life was not easy, but life was even harder for the Jews and the Christians because of the many special restrictions placed on them. For example, for a time such a very heavy annual tax was imposed upon the Jews in Jerusalem that many of them were forced to leave the city.

There was also little building and renovation done in Palestine. Some of the Christian churches, for example, gradually fell into decay because the impoverished Christian community was unable to maintain them, while others were confiscated by the Muslims. And, whereas in Egypt the Mamluks built rich, beautiful structures, in Palestine they took far less interest. They did keep the Dome of the Rock and the al-Aqsa Mosque in repair, however; and they also built some of the gates of the Haram esh-Sharif, as well as the arcades which lead to the platform of the Dome of the Rock. In addition, the Mamluks built four handsome madrasahs in the city, which were a combination of mosque and school.

Fourteenth Century

Pilgrims and visitors — both Jews and Christians — continued to come to the Holy Land. Jacques of Verona, an Augustinian monk, came in 1335. In his *Liber Peregrinationis* he explains how he discovered that the Jews were able to recount the history of the places he visited, because they had knowledge which had been passed on to them by their forefathers.

The Custody of the Holy Land. Already in about 1219 Saint Francis of Assisi had joined the Crusaders. In Egypt he visited al-Kamil, then the Ayubid sultan, and from then on the Franciscan Order showed a special interest in the East and in the Holy Land. Accordingly, in 1342 the Pope at Rome officially charged the

The Franciscan Dominus flevit Chapel, situated about halfway down the direct descent of the west side of the Mount of Olives, provides a panoramic view of Jerusalem across the Kidron Valley. The chapel marks the site traditionally said to be the place where Jesus wept over the city.

Order with the guardianship of the holy places — called "The Custody of the Holy Land" — in the name of worldwide Christianity. Although the Franciscan brothers individually maintained their founder's rule of poverty, the Order itself received much financial backing for its work, and thus was able to purchase many sacred sites in Palestine. The Order also provided places of hospitality for Christian pilgrims. (Note: Today the Franciscan Order is recognized by the Roman Catholic Church as maintaining the custody of the Holy Land. It uses as its symbol a form of the Maltese cross, with four small crosses between its arms.)

In 1350 a German pastor named Ludolph von Suchem wrote a book about his travels in the Holy Land. When he visited the Church of the Holy Sepulcher he was amazed that the Saracens had not harmed the tombs of the Crusader leaders, Godfrey de Bouillon and his brother, King Baldwin. At Hebron he visited "a fair church, wherein is the double cave wherein the three patriarchs, Abraham, Isaac, and Jacob, are buried, together with their wives." The Saracens hold the church especially sacred, says von Suchem, but they allow the Jews to enter — for a price. At Bethlehem he saw the Church of the Nativity and the monastery in which Jerome, Paula, and Eustochium once lived; he discovered that a fee was collected at this church, too, but in this instance was demanded of everyone — not just Jews.

Fifteenth Century

In 1488 Rabbi Obadiah da Bertinoro, a renowned scholar, made the pilgrimage from Italy and stayed in Jerusalem to serve as the spiritual leader of the small Jewish community. He wrote that Jerusalem was "for the most part desolate and in ruins" and "not surrounded by walls." The population was estimated at about 4,000 families; of these, only about 70 were Jewish families, and they were of the poorest class. The Jews were forbidden to enter the Temple enclosure, but the Rabbi was able to visit the Western Wall of the Temple area. He was greatly impressed by its large, thick stones, which were such as he had never before seen in an old building either in Rome or in any other country.

In 1480 and again in 1484 a German Dominican monk named Felix Fabri visited the country and wrote a report called *Evagatorium in Terram Sanctam*. About Jerusalem he noted that "there are scattered throughout the city many chapels of heretics [i.e., Christian sects other than the Latin], many Saracen mosques, Jewish synagogues, and Samaritan tabernacles." He learned that there were more than 500 Jews there, and more than 1,000 Christians of various sects and countries, but very few of the Latin sect.

In 1491-1492 a Christian pilgrim from Bohemia named Martin Kabtanik visited Palestine and wrote a book called *Journey to Jerusalem*. He described both Christians and Jews in Jerusalem as living in great poverty:

> There are not many Christians but there are many Jews, and these the Muslims persecute in various ways. Christians and Jews go about in Jerusalem in clothes considered fit only for wandering beggars. The Muslims know that the Jews think and even say that this is the Holy Land which has been promised to them and that those Jews who dwell there are regarded as holy by Jews elsewhere, because, in spite of all the troubles and sorrows inflicted on them by the Muslims, they refuse to leave the land.

In spite of such deprivations suffered during the Mamluk period by both Jews and Christians, it has been remarked that during this time the Jews actually fared better than they had under the Crusaders, and the Christians were also better off than the Muslims had been under them.

F. OTTOMAN PERIOD (1517-1918 C.E.)

The last of the great empires to be established by the Turkish peoples was that of the Ottoman Turks, who were originally driven from their home in Central Asia by the Mongol invasion, but who in their further push to the West were at least in part responding to the Crusaders' attacks, which for two centuries had ravaged the Muslim world of which they had become a part. In 1453 Muhammad II the Conqueror (1451-1481) took Constantinople. In 1517 Selim I

Now walled up in the eastern wall of the Temple area, the Golden Gate may represent the Beautiful Gate of earlier times (Acts 3:2, 10), because the Greek word meaning "beautiful" sounds something like the Latin word aurea, meaning "golden," and could have given rise to the present name.

(1512-1520) — whose ideal was to unite the Muslim East rather than to fight against the Christian West — defeated the Mamluks and took Syria, Palestine, Egypt, and Arabia. For the next 400 years Palestine was an Ottoman domain, divided into five separately controlled districts usually ruled by Turkish governors called pashas.

Sixteenth Century

Suleiman I the Magnificent. The Ottoman administration was at its best in its earliest years, particularly under Sultan Suleiman I the Magnificent (1520-1566), son of Selim I. In Palestine his major work (accomplished from 1538 to 1542) was the rebuilding of the walls of Jerusalem; in fact, the walls which surround the Old City today are the walls of Suleiman, practically unchanged. On them are still a number of his inscriptions; there is one, for example, at the Jaffa Gate with a date in the year 945 of the Muslim calendar (1538/1539 C.E.). Because he basically built over the layers or on top of the debris of earlier walls, for the most part the line of his walls probably follows that of the walls of Hadrian's Aelia Capitolina. This assumption is best proved at the Damascus Gate on the north side of the Old City, where a side arch of Hadrian's gate and some Herodian masonry as well have been uncovered along the side of the moat, which one crosses on a modern bridge. Suleiman I also replaced the mosaics on the exterior of the Dome of the Rock with faience tiles in blue, white, green, and yellow; and these, restored in the present century, give the dome its present splendid appearance.

The Damascus Gate in the Old City of Jerusalem provides access to what was probably the main north-south street in the Roman city of Jerusalem built by Hadrian after the Second Revolt (132-135 C.E.). At this time the city was known by Hadrian's family name, Aelia Capitolina.

It was the policy of the Ottoman rulers to allow Jewish immigration, and in the sixteenth century thousands of Jews came to Palestine, especially ones who were fleeing from Christian persecution in Europe. Many were from Spain and Portugal, where the Jewish communities had been expelled in 1492 and 1496 respectively; others came from Central and Eastern Europe. In contrast with the native Arabic-speaking Jews of Palestine, the newcomers spoke other languages. The Jews from Spain and Portugal, called Sephardim, spoke Ladino, a medieval Spanish amplified with Hebrew words and written in Hebrew characters. The Jews from Central and Eastern Europe, called Ashkenazim, spoke Yiddish, a medieval German amplified with Hebrew words and written in Hebrew characters.

At this time the main centers of Jewish life in Palestine were Jerusalem, Safad, Tiberias, and Hebron. At Jerusalem the Jewish inhabitants, numbering between 1,000 and 1,500, lived in three quarters which today constitute the so-called Jewish Quarter of the Old City. The largest community, at Safad, numbered about 10,000 Jews.

Rabbi Isaac Luria, who was born in Jerusalem in 1534 and died in Safad in 1573, made Safad and nearby Meron the chief centers of the Jewish movement of mysticism known as Cabalism. He was called ha-Ari (the Lion); and the two oldest synagogues in Safad today, which are associated with his work, are known as Ha-Ari of the Sephardim and Ha-Ari of the Ashkenazim. Rabbi Joseph Karo, a Spanish Jew, was a member of Rabbi Luria's Cabalist circle and wrote in 1563 the Shulhan Aruch (Arranged Table), which has become the standard codification of Talmudic law for orthodox Jews throughout the world. In Safad the Maran Beth Joseph Synagogue is named after him.

In the middle of the sixteenth century the term *Via Dolorosa* began to be used to name the route along which (it is traditionally thought) Jesus was led from the Praetorium to Golgotha. It is said to begin at the northwest corner of the Temple area (the assumption being that the Antonia fortress was the place of the trial before Pilate) and end at the Church of the Holy Sepulcher. The sites commemorated along the way varied in number and place until the fourteen stations known today were standardized in the middle of the nineteenth century.

Seventeenth Century

In the seventeenth century the rule of the sultans from Istanbul grew lax — so lax that, in Palestine, the Bedouins and Druzes sacked both Safad and Tiberias. Palestine had other troubles as well: local Turkish officials imposed enormous taxes, the land was neglected, and natural disasters also took their toll.

The situation of the Jews was described by George Sandys, son of the Archbishop of York, who visited Palestine in 1611 and wrote in his *Travailes:* "In

Transformed by tourists and peddlers, the Via Dolorosa doesn't resemble "The Way of Sorrow." This is traditionally assumed to be the route Jesus took to Calvary — an assumption based on the hypothesis that Jesus' trial took place at the Antonia fortress at the northwest corner of the Temple area.

their Land they live as strangers, hated by those amongst whom they dwell, open to all oppression and deprivation, which they bear with patience beyond all belief, despised and beaten." Another observer was Ignatius von Rheinfelden, a Franciscan monk from Germany who visited the land in 1656 and wrote in his book, *New Jerusalemite Pilgrimages:* "In Jerusalem there also live many Jews who came from all over the world to await the coming of the Messiah and to welcome him. . . . Some Jews who can afford it leave instructions in their wills that after their death their bodies should be transferred to Jerusalem and buried in the Valley of Jehoshaphat."

At this time there was intense rivalry among the Christian sects. The Church of the Holy Sepulcher was especially an object of contention. Henry Maundrell, an English ecclesiastic who was a pilgrim in 1697, wrote of the "unchristian fury and animosity, especially between the Greeks and Latins," which characterized the sectarian struggle for "the command and appropriation of the Holy Sepulchre." With greater appreciation Maundrell speaks of the Armenian Christians, who had their own tract of land (the present Armenian Quarter) and a church with two splendid altars — the Church of St. James. Supposedly built on the site of the house of Saint James the Less, the brother of Jesus and first bishop of the Jerusalem church, this church also commemorates Saint James the Great, the son of Zebedee and brother of John.

Eighteenth Century

In the eighteenth century the economic and political situation in Palestine only grew worse. Yet in 1701 Rabbi Yehuda ha-Hassid (Judah the Pious) arrived from Poland with a large body of his students and their families, and in 1751 the Swedish traveler Frederick Hasselquist noted the yearly arrival of thousands of Christians as well as Jews.

In 1757 the Ottoman government found it necessary to draw up a document called *The Status Quo in the Holy Places*, which prescribed the several rights of possession and worship of the different Christian denominations in the Church of the Holy Sepulcher. The determinations made at that time are essentially the same as those which apply today. Six Christian communions share in the official use of the church. The three major ones are the Latin (represented by the Franciscan Custody of the Holy Land), the Greek Orthodox, and the Armenian Orthodox; the three minor ones are the Coptic, the Syrian, and the Ethiopian. Under an arrangement drawn up even earlier — in the thirteenth century — a Muslim Arab family, Nusseibeh, holds the keys for opening and closing the church.

al-Jazzar. Toward the close of the eighteenth century a Bedouin sheikh named Zaher el-Amir obtained rights over Galilee from the Ottomans, and annexed other regions until he ruled almost the entire country, establishing Acre as his capital. There he was succeeded by Ahmad, surnamed al-Jazzar ("the Butcher," so called for his cruelty), who also governed most of the land from 1775 to 1804. He built up and fortified the city, and also erected the large Mosque of al-Jazzar, using for its arcades a number of marble columns brought from Caesarea on the coast. In 1799 Napoleon Bonaparte advanced from Egypt, but Acre, assisted by the British fleet, withstood his siege, and Napoleon abandoned his Near Eastern campaign.

Nineteenth Century

In the first half of the nineteenth century Palestine had become almost completely impoverished, and its population was at its lowest number, estimated at not more than 250,000 altogether. A Protestant theologian named Felix Bovet visited the land in 1858 and wrote:

> The Christians who conquered the Land of Israel did not know how to hold it and it was never anything more to them than a battleground and a graveyard. The Saracens who took it from them also left and it was then taken by the Turks and the Ottomans who are still there. They have made a desert of it where it is scarcely possible to walk without fear. Even the Arabs who dwell there do so as temporary sojourners.

In the second half of the nineteenth century various people came to Palestine from the West; thus began the efforts to repair the damages of long-standing neglect in the country. The Jews' return to the land, called the First Aliyah (literally meaning "ascent" or "going up"), was gradual. One of the first to come was Sir Moses Montefiore of England, who made his first pilgrimage to the Holy Land in 1836 and his last, at the age of 91, in 1875. In 1855 he received from the Sultan in Constantinople the right to acquire land outside the walls of Jerusalem and to repair the tomb of Rachel at Bethlehem. In 1860 he completed the first Jewish quarter outside the walls of the Old City; the windmill he built there is still standing.

As more Jews entered the land, development increased. In 1870 they founded the Mikveh Israel Agricultural School, which today is on the outskirts of Tel Aviv. In 1878 they established a farming settlement called Petah Tikvah (Gateway of Hope) — today a town of 85,000 inhabitants 16 km (10 mi) from Tel Aviv. Pressures upon the Jews in Europe — particularly the pogroms in Russia in the 1880's — sent many more immigrants to Palestine, and thus more agricultural villages were founded: Rishon le-Zion (First in Zion), Nes Ziona (Banner of Zion), and others — seventeen in all by 1900. Societies sprang up in the Dispersion called Hovevei Zion (Lovers of Zion), and there was a movement called Bilu, which created its name from the initial letters of a Hebrew slogan, "O House of Jacob, come and let us go forth!"

The European powers of Christendom also took a fresh interest in the Holy Land in the latter half of the nineteenth century. In 1852 the Turkish sultan settled conflicts between France, which supported the Latin Church, and Russia, which supported the Greek Orthodox Church. In the Crimean War, England, France, and Turkey defeated Russia; and in the peace treaty signed after the war

This is the Church of St. Mary Magdalene, which represents the great interest of the Russian Orthodox Church in the Holy Land. Situated on the lower slope of the Mount of Olives, it is below the Dominus flevit Chapel and above the Garden of Gethsemane.

in 1856 various special privileges were granted to non-Muslim communities. In spite of the outcome of the war, Russian influence continued to be strong. In the latter part of the century, for example, a huge Russian compound was built on top of the Mount of Olives, including a church and a very tall tower commemorating the Ascension, a hospital, and hostels established for Russian pilgrims. In addition, the Russian Church of St. Mary Magdalene was built on the lower slope of the same mount as it descends toward the Kidron Valley. There is also a Russian Alexander Hospice which is built over the remains of some very ancient stone walls and columns not far from the Church of the Holy Sepulcher.

In 1898 the German Kaiser Wilhelm II made a formal visit to Jerusalem, and the Germans soon after began to erect some of the major buildings still to be seen in the city. The German Lutheran Church of the Redeemer was built on the nearest available site to the Church of the Holy Sepulcher. On Mount Zion (the southwestern hill outside the present wall of the Old City), the emperor presented a plot of land to the German Catholic Society of the Holy Land, and the Church of the Dormition (marking the place where Mary, Jesus' mother, supposedly died) was soon built there, as was a Zion convent, occupied by the Benedictines from Beuron. Named after the wife of Wilhelm II, the Augusta Victoria Hospital, with its imposing square tower, was built on the ridge between the Mount of Olives and Mount Scopus.

Groups and individuals from various other places also began enterprises in Palestine — some in a purely humanitarian spirit, others in an attempt to convert the Muslims and Jews to Christianity. A single example among many is the American Colony on Nablus Road. This was founded as a charitable mission by a Chicago lawyer named Horatio G. Spafford, who went to Jerusalem with his family in 1881. Still well-known as the American Colony Hotel, it occupies a former pasha's palace.

Zionism. In the long and terrible story of anti-Semitism in the world, the pogroms in Russia in 1881-1882 were a particularly black chapter. They perhaps inspired a Jewish physician in Odessa named Leon Pinsker to publish in 1882 a pamphlet entitled *Auto-Emancipation.* In it he described the Jew as a "stranger everywhere, wanted nowhere, and having no home of his own," and argued that the only solution would be "the creation of a Jewish nationality . . . living upon its own soil."

But Pinsker was not the only one to reach this conclusion. In 1894 in France, Alfred Dreyfus, a French army officer of Jewish descent, was convicted of treason for which a non-Jewish superior officer was actually guilty, and, in a trial marked by blatant displays of anti-Semitism, was sentenced to Devil's Island. Theodor Herzl (1860-1904), a Jew born in Budapest, covered the trial as a journalist for a Vienna newspaper. Appalled by what he saw, he, like Pinsker, realized the importance of establishing a Jewish state. Acting on this belief, in 1896 he wrote *Judenstaat (The Jewish State)*, and in 1897 he called together the First Zionist Congress in Basel, the first official, worldwide gathering of Jews since their Dispersion. At the congress it was declared that the "aim of Zionism is to create for the Jewish people a publicly and legally assured home in Palestine." To reach this goal they established the World Zionist Organization, which adopted a national anthem, *Hatikvah* ("The Hope") and what has become the flag of Israel (the star of David against a white background horizontally bordered with two blue stripes).

Additional Reading on the American Colony

Vester, Bertha Spafford. *Our Jerusalem: An American Family in the Holy City, 1881-1949.* Lebanon: Middle East Export Press, 1950. The story of the American colony, a community center with its doors open to all of Jerusalem's inhabitants — Muslim, Christian, and Jew. Begun under Turkish rule, it survived through two world wars, the period of the British mandate, and the tumultuous events of 1948.

Additional Reading on Zionism

Buber, Martin. *On Zion: The History of an Idea.* New York: Schocken Books, 1973. A sympathetic presentation of Zionism by the noted Jewish philosopher.

Rabinowicz, Oskar K. *Arnold Toynbee on Judaism and Zionism: A Critique.* London: W. H. Allen, 1974. One of the leaders of the Zionist movement in Czechoslovakia exhaustively analyzes Toynbee's discussion of Zionism in contrast with assimilationism, and Toynbee's explanation of Zionism as a movement comparable to Nazism and inspired by the spirit of western nationalism.

Sandmel, Samuel. *The Several Israels.* New York: Ktav Publishing House, 1971. Includes a delineation of Zionism, and contains an essay on religion and modern man.

Midstream is a current Zionist journal published by The Theodor Herzl Foundation, 515 Park Ave., New York, N.Y. 10022. The foundation is an educational agency that promotes the study and discussion of problems confronting Jews today.

IV. TWENTIETH-CENTURY ISRAEL: From British Rule to Independence

Impelled and financially supported by the Zionist movement, the Second Aliyah, the second great wave of Jewish immigration to Palestine, began in 1904. The Jewish National Fund, an agency of the World Zionist Organization, purchased land from Arab and Turkish landowners, held it on behalf of the Jewish people, and made it available without charge or rented it to settlers. In 1909 the first kibbutz (collective settlement), called Degania, was established on such land just south of the Sea of Galilee; in the same year some residents of Jaffa moved to the sandhills to the north and developed a suburb which grew to be Tel Aviv. Already in 1880 a young medical student named Eliezer Ben Yehuda arrived in Jaffa and worked unceasingly to revive the Hebrew language. In 1904 he became the first chairman of the Hebrew Language Council; under its influence Hebrew became the principal language of the Yishuv, as the Jewish community in Palestine was at this time called. By 1914 the Jewish community numbered approximately 85,000.

Near the outbreak of the First World War in 1914, Turkey joined Germany against the Allied Powers, and when they could the British moved against the Turks in Palestine. In 1917 General Edmund Allenby pushed into Palestine from the south; on November 14 he took Jaffa, and then marched on Jerusalem. A week later, on November 21, he captured the prominent height of Nebi Samwil, which almost overlooks the city, since it is only 8 km (5 mi) away to the northwest. On December 9 Jerusalem surrendered, and Allenby entered the city on foot, out of respect. In the fall of 1918 he completed the conquest of the Turkish armies at the famous battlefield of Megiddo, and Turkey capitulated.

Because the end of the war marked the end of the Ottoman empire, the League of Nations gave Great Britain the mandate for Palestine on July 24, 1922.

A. THE PERIOD OF THE BRITISH MANDATE (1918-1948 C.E.)

On November 2, 1917, about five weeks before the fall of Jerusalem to Allenby, the British government issued the Balfour Declaration. This document declared:

His Majesty's Government view with favour the establishment in Palestine of a national home for the Jewish people, and will use their best endeavours to facilitate the achievement of this object, it being clearly understood that nothing shall be done which may prejudice the civil and religious rights of the existing non-Jewish communities in Palestine, or the rights and political status enjoyed by Jews in any other country.

The text of this declaration was incorporated in the mandate given to Britain by the League of Nations, and thus the British government was held responsible "for placing the country under such political, administrative and economic conditions as will secure the establishment of the Jewish national home." The Jewish community was to be represented by the Jewish Agency for Palestine, an organization recognized by the World Zionist Organization.

At the outset the plan for a Jewish homeland in Palestine met with approval from those who at the time appeared to be the leaders of the Arab world. These were Husein, Grand Sherif of Mecca and later King of Hejaz, and his son, the Emir Faisal. (The Emir, who later became the King of Iraq, was the chief spokesman for the Arabs at the Peace Conference at Versailles at the end of the First World War, and had Lawrence of Arabia as his adviser.) After meeting with Jewish leaders in London, Faisal issued a statement which was published in *The Times* for December 12, 1918. He said: "The two main branches of the Semitic family, Arabs and Jews, understand one another.... Arabs are not jealous of Zionist Jews, and intend to give them fair play; and the Zionist Jews have assured the Nationalist Arabs of their intention to see that they, too, have fair play in their respective areas."

In the next year Faisal signed an agreement with Chaim Weizmann, then head of the World Zionist Organization and later the first President of Israel, approving of Jewish immigration to and settlement in Palestine, provided that an Arab state was set up in the surrounding territories. In a letter dated March 3, 1919, to the American Jewish leader Justice Felix Frankfurter, Faisal declared: "We Arabs... look with the deepest sympathy on the Zionist Movement. Our deputation here in Paris is fully acquainted with the proposals submitted yesterday by the Zionist Organization to the Peace Conference.... We will do our best... to help them through; we will wish the Jews a most hearty welcome home."

But other and contrary voices were heard very soon. A General Syrian Congress met in July 1919, claiming to represent Muslims, Christians, and Jews, and stated: "We oppose the pretensions of Zionists to create a Jewish Commonwealth in the southern part of Syria, known as Palestine, and oppose Zionist migration to any part of our country; for we do not acknowledge their title but consider them a grave peril to our people from the national, economical, and political points of view." In addition, in 1920 there were Arab attacks upon two Jewish settlements in the north of Palestine, and a Palestine Arab Congress of Muslims and Christians rejected all Jewish claims to a place in the land, insisting that Palestine belonged exclusively to the Muslim and Christian worlds.

During the period of the British mandate are reckoned three further waves of Jewish immigration to Palestine: the Third Aliyah, which occurred immediately after the First World War when the war and its aftermath had brought great suffering to Jews, especially those in Eastern Europe; the Fourth Aliyah (1924-1926), which occurred when conditions in Poland caused many to leave; and the Fifth Aliyah, which occurred when many fled from Germany and other countries in Central Europe because of Hitler's appointment as chancellor (in January 1933) and the rise of National Socialism in Germany.

Unfortunately, Great Britain was not consistent in its handling of the various immigrations. At certain times Jewish immigration to Palestine was allowed; at other times it was severely restricted, and land purchase was prevented. In fact, in May 1939 the same British government (headed by Neville Chamberlain) that attempted the appeasement of Germany at Munich also sought to keep the Arab powers from alignment with Berlin and Rome, and issued the so-called White Paper, which some at the time described as a Palestine Munich. This document allowed only 75,000 Jewish immigrants to enter the country over a five-year period, after which no more would be permitted to enter, except with Arab consent.

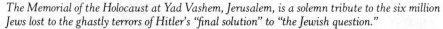

The Memorial of the Holocaust at Yad Vashem, Jerusalem, is a solemn tribute to the six million Jews lost to the ghastly terrors of Hitler's "final solution" to "the Jewish question."

The Holocaust. This severe restriction of immigration came at the very time that the horror of the Holocaust, as it is properly called, enveloped the Jews of Europe. During the Second World War (from 1939 to 1945), in Germany and the countries they dominated the Nazis systematically murdered nearly six million Jews — men, women, and children — out of the sixteen million Jews in the world. At Yad Vashem in Jerusalem is the solemn memorial to the martyrs and heroes of those terrible days, and the most extensive documentation of what happened.

Unfortunately, the doors to Palestine opened no wider for the refugees from this terror and for the survivors of the death camps. Although the British tried to keep them out, many illegal immigrants came anyway. The Jewish Haganah (Defense), organized originally in 1920 for protection against Arab attacks, helped them in every way it could, resorting to smuggling and sabotage, while two underground groups — the Irgun Zvai Leumi (National Military Organization) and the even more extreme Lohamei Herut Israel (Israel Freedom Fighters, also known as the Stern Group, from its founder Avraham Stern, whose underground name was Yair) — turned for a time to more violent action. Meanwhile, Arab terrorism continued against the Jews in Palestine.

The Termination of the Mandate. Because of this state of affairs, in February 1947 the British government turned over the Palestine mandate and all of its apparently unsolvable problems to the United Nations, the successor (in 1945) to the League of Nations. Later that year, on November 29, 1947, the General Assembly of the United Nations voted to divide Palestine into independent Jewish and Arab states, with Jerusalem in an internationalized zone. At the time, according to the figures of the mandatory government, there were in Palestine 1,200,000 Arabs, 650,000 Jews, and 150,000 "others."

Additional Reading on the Holocaust

The Holocaust. Yad Vashem, Jerusalem: Martyrs' and Heroes' Remembrance Authority, 1977. A factual text with appalling pictures.

Holocaust Studies Newsletter. National Institute on the Holocaust, P.O. Box 2147, Philadelphia, PA 19103. 1977-. Note that the first graduate program in Holocaust studies in the United States has been established at Temple University, Philadelphia 19122, and operates in cooperation with the Department of Holocaust Studies at the Hebrew University in Jerusalem.

Knopp, Josephine, ed. *Second Philadelphia Conference on the Holocaust — February 16-18, 1977.* Proceedings of a conference with the theme "Humanizing America: A Post-Holocaust Imperative." (Obtain by writing Suite 500, 260 S. 15th St., Philadelphia, PA 19102.)

Littell, Franklin H., and Hubert G. Locke, eds. *The German Church Struggle and the Holocaust.* Detroit: Wayne State University Press, 1974. A series of papers from the First International Scholars' Conference held on this subject in 1970.

Shoah: A Review of Holocaust Studies and Commemorations. A joint project of the National Jewish Conference Center (250 W. 57th St., Suite 923, New York, N.Y. 10029) and the University of Bridgeport, Bridgeport, Conn.

Roughly, the territory was divided this way: the Jewish state would consist of the land in eastern Galilee, and the land in the Negev beginning at the Gulf of Aqabah and running along the coast northward to Haifa and Acre; the Arab state would consist of the land in western Galilee, the land on the west bank of the Jordan and that running down through the central highlands of Samaria and Judea as far as Beersheba, and the land on the Gaza coast and inland paralleling a part of the Israeli Negev. The proposed Jerusalem district, to be under international administration, included Bethlehem.

In the United Nations thirty-three members voted for the partition and thirteen voted against it; there were ten abstentions. Both the United States and the Soviet Union voted for the partition. The Zionist Congress had already voted to accept the plan of partition, but in the same United Nations session which voted for the resolution the Arab delegates declared that their states would resist the plan, using force against it if necessary. In fact, the Arab resistance began the next day — November 30, 1947 — and continued into 1948.

The British announced that their mandate would terminate on May 15, 1948. One day early, on May 14, the British High Commissioner, Alan Cunningham, and his staff sailed away from Palestine.

At 4:00 in the afternoon of that day, just before the start of the Jewish Sabbath at sunset, David Ben-Gurion, Chairman of the Jewish Agency for Palestine, read to the Vaad Leumi (National Council) of the Yishuv in Tel Aviv a Proclamation of Independence of the State of Israel:

> Eretz Israel [the Land of Israel] was the birthplace of the Jewish people. Here their spiritual, religious and political identity was shaped. Here they first attained to statehood, created cultural values of national and universal significance and gave to the world the eternal Book of Books.
>
> After being forcibly exiled from their land, the people kept faith with it throughout their Dispersion and never ceased to pray and hope for their return to it and for the restoration in it of their political freedom. . . .

After referring to the action of the General Assembly of the United Nations, the Proclamation continued:

> This recognition by the United Nations of the right of the Jewish people to establish their State is irrevocable.
>
> This right is the natural right of the Jewish people to be masters of their own fate, like all other nations, in their own sovereign State.

Thus, its independence declared, the State of Israel was established. It was pledged that Israel would accept Jewish immigrants and exiles, but would offer peace and friendship to all neighboring states and would support the common goal of the advancement of the entire Middle East.

The proclamation was dated on the Sabbath eve, the fifth day of Iyar, in the year 5708 of the Jewish calendar, corresponding to the fourteenth day of May, 1948 C.E.

B. THE INDEPENDENT STATE OF ISRAEL (FROM 1948 C.E.): A STORMY BEGINNING

At 5:16 p.m. on the day of the Proclamation of Independence of the State of Israel, the United States recognized the new state; the Soviet Union was the next to grant recognition.

The War of Independence in 1948. On the day after the Proclamation of Independence — May 15, 1948 — Egyptian warplanes bombed Tel Aviv; and the regular armies of Egypt, Jordan, Lebanon, Syria, and Iraq, as well as a contingent from Saudi Arabia, also attacked the new state. In Cairo, Azzam Pasha, Secretary-General of the Arab League, declared: "This will be a war of extermination and a momentous massacre which will be spoken of like the Mongolian massacres and Crusades."

This was the War of Independence for Israel, which pitted its population of 650,000 against the combined population of the Arab lands — more than 40 million people. When it was ended in 1949 by separate armistice agreements with Egypt, Jordan, Lebanon, and Syria, the territory of Israel extended from the old borders of Lebanon and Syria in the north to the Gulf of Aqabah in the south; the Kingdom of Jordan held the West Bank of the Jordan, an area which reached the southern Jezreel Valley, extended at one point to within 14 km (9 mi) of the Mediterranean coast, and included the Old City of Jerusalem as well as Bethlehem and Hebron. The total area of Israel was 20,700 sq km or 7,993 sq mi, its newly established borders remaining the same until 1967.

In early 1949 the first Knesset, the parliament of Israel, was elected: Chaim Weizmann was elected the first president, and David Ben-Gurion became the prime minister. One of the first laws passed was the Law of Return, which, written in the spirit of the Proclamation of Independence, assured the right of every Jew in the world to settle in Israel and be its citizen. In response, waves of immigrants came — from Central and Eastern Europe; from Arab countries in Iraq, Yemen, and North Africa; from Western Europe and North and South

---

Additional Reading on the Return to Palestine and the Establishment of the State of Israel

Uris, Leon. *Exodus.* Garden City: Doubleday, 1958. In this historical novel, Dov Landau, a Jewish boy of Warsaw, lives through the massacre of the Jews in Warsaw, survives Auschwitz, escapes the British detention camp on Cyprus, and fights with the Jewish forces in Palestine. As the book closes in mingled triumph and tragedy, he reads the ritual of the celebration of Passover in the free State of Israel.

America; and, when allowed, from the Soviet Union. In twenty-four years —
from 1948 to 1972 — the total Jewish population in Israel thus increased from
650,000 to 2,723,000.

The Suez War in 1956. Although the armistice at the end of the War of
Independence was supposedly supervised by the United Nations, Israel came to
feel that this supervision was either biased against them or ineffective. They no
doubt felt this way because Arab hostility continued unchecked; in fact, in the
1950's Arab guerrillas were making raids deep into Israeli territory and
terrorizing the population. Egypt also posed a threat: under President Gamal
Nasser there was a massive armament program, and Egypt seized the Suez
Canal, which previously had been controlled by international interests through
the Suez Canal Company. In addition, Egypt established alliances with Syria and
Jordan, which made Israel feel surrounded by enemies.

Under David Ben-Gurion as prime minister and with Moshe Dayan as
field commander, Israel attacked Egypt on October 29, 1956. At the same time
Britain and France, opposed to the nationalization of the Suez Canal by Egypt,
sent their war planes. The Israeli forces broke a blockade of the Gulf of Aqabah
and drove the Egyptian army out of Gaza, while French and British troops
occupied the Suez Canal area.

The United States and Russia, however, together constrained the French
and British to withdraw and allow the Suez Canal to return to unilateral Egyptian
control; meanwhile, Israel also withdrew, but only after securing guarantees from
the United Nations ensuring freedom of navigation in the Gulf of Aqabah and
freedom from guerrilla attacks from the Gaza Strip. The "guarantees," however,
proved to be only temporary.

The Six-Day War in 1967. Guerrilla attacks continued, and by 1967 it was
evident that Israel was again being encircled by Arab armies intent upon a new
war. Egypt drove the United Nations Emergency Force from Sinai, Gaza, and
the entrance to the Gulf of Aqabah, and then blockaded the gulf. Announcing
the blockade in a speech on May 22, President Nasser said: "Taking such action
means that we are ready to enter war with Israel.... The battle will be a general
one and our basic objective will be to destroy Israel."

On June 5 — under Levi Eshkol as prime minister and with
Major-General Moshe Dayan as defense minister and Yitzchak Rabin as chief of
staff — Israel attacked. With fighting already raging on that day between Israel
and the Egyptians in Sinai, Eshkol sent a message through United Nations
officials to Amman, the capital of Jordan, asking King Hussein to stay out of the
war. But on the same day Jordanian artillery and ground forces attacked
Jerusalem. In quick response Israeli forces — some even withdrawn from the

Two men stop to pray at the Western Wall (Wailing Wall) of the Temple area. The great drafted blocks in the wall's lower courses are those of the enclosure wall constructed by Herod the Great. As the tangible remains of the Second Temple, they are of special significance to Jews.

battle in Sinai — were moved to Jerusalem. On June 7 they fought their way into the Old City through St. Stephen's Gate and reached the Western Wall (the so-called Wailing Wall). Thus for the first time in nineteen centuries the entire city of Jerusalem was in Jewish hands. And at the end of the week, when a cease-fire ended the war, Israel was in control of new territories with more than one million Arab inhabitants. In addition to East Jerusalem and the Old City, these were the West Bank (basically equivalent to biblical Judea and Samaria), the Gaza Strip, the Sinai Desert, and the Golan Heights.

The Yom Kippur War in 1973. On October 6, 1973, the Jewish Day of Atonement (Yom Kippur), Egypt and Syria jointly attacked Israel, their ranks soon reinforced by contingents from Jordan, Iraq, Morocco, and some other Arab states. Again a cease-fire was established, and the Israeli, Egyptian, and Syrian forces were separated under the supervision of the United Nations. After this conflict Israel occupied even more territory in the Golan Heights and the Sinai.

Egypt's Peace Initiative. At the end of the Sabbath day on Saturday, November 19, 1977 — approximately thirty years after Egyptian warplanes bombed Tel Aviv on the day after the inauguration of the new State of Israel — President Anwar Sadat of Egypt flew to Tel Aviv's Ben Gurion Airport and proceeded to Jerusalem. There, on Sunday, November 20, he addressed the Knesset and declared Egypt's desire for peace, to which Prime Minister Menachem Begin of Israel responded with a similar expression of Israel's desire for peace. President Sadat also performed symbolically significant acts: he prayed in the Muslim al-Aqsa Mosque and visited the Christian Church of the Holy Sepulcher. Was it the beginning of a new day?

Jewish settlements are now established on the heights on the east side of the Sea of Galilee, an area presently occupied but not annexed by Israel. (The Golan Heights are on the far side.)

Additional Reading on the History of Israel

Bahat, Dan, ed. *Twenty Centuries of Jewish Life in the Holy Land: The Forgotten Generations.* 2nd ed. Jerusalem: The Israel Economist, 1976. Historical summaries, quotations, and illustrations for each of the centuries.

Dimont, Max I. *Jews, God and History.* New York: Simon and Schuster (hardcover); New York: New American Library, Signet Book, 1962. This is a lively history of the amazing 4,000-year survival of the Jews, who have lived in the context of six civilizations, most of which have passed away while the Jews continue. Speculative in its reconstruction of many events in biblical history.

Dodd, C. H., and M. E. Sales. *Israel and the Arab World.* London: Routledge and Kegan Paul, 1970. Selected documents, together with a guide to further reading, and topics for discussion.

Eban, Abba. *My People: The Story of the Jews.* New York: Behrman House and Random House, 1968. An eloquently phrased account of events through the Six-Day War in 1967, written by the man who was then Israel's minister for foreign affairs.

Kollek, Teddy, and Moshe Pearlman. *Pilgrims to the Holy Land.* London: Weidenfeld and Nicolson, 1970. Traces the long line of pilgrims — Jewish, Christian, and Muslim — that visited Palestine through the centuries, and includes their reports about the land.

Learsi, Rufus. *Israel: A History of the Jewish People.* Cleveland: World Publishing, Meridian Books, 1966. A detailed history of events through the First and Second World Wars.

Parkes, James. *A History of Palestine from 135 A.D. to Modern Times.* New York: Oxford University Press, 1949. A standard work, revised as *Whose Land? A History of the Peoples of Palestine.* Baltimore: Penguin Books, 1970.

Polk, William R. *The United States and the Arab World.* Cambridge: Harvard University Press, 1965. Recognizes the quest of the Arabs for identity and dignity.

Sachar, Abram Leon. *A History of the Jews.* 5th ed. rev. New York: Knopf, 1965. A standard one-volume history.

Note: the quotations from various documents used in the preceding section can all be verified in the above sources.

See also:

Ben-Gurion, David. *Israel: A Personal History.* New York: Funk and Wagnalls, 1971.

————. *Memoirs.* Ed. Thomas R. Branstein. New York: World Publishing, 1970.

First Fruits: A Harvest of Twenty-Five Years of Israeli Writing. Philadelphia: Jewish Publication Society, 1973.

Meir, Golda. *My Life.* New York: Putnam, 1975.

Michener, James. *The Source.* New York: Random House, 1965.

PART THREE

TODAY'S ISRAEL: *Its Complexity and Diversity*

This poverty-stricken village in Wadi Fara illustrates the pitiful condition of many Arab refugees, a problem that will continue to strain Arab-Israeli relations until it is justly resolved.

I. ITS CHALLENGE:
Establishing a Just Peace

When Egyptian President Sadat addressed the Knesset in Jerusalem in 1977, he stated that the existence of Israel was an "established fact," affirmed that Israel should be able "to live within its borders secure from any attack," and said, "We welcome you among us." At the same time he reiterated the fundamental Arab position that the establishment of peace depended upon the withdrawal of Israel from all Arab territory, including Arab Jerusalem, captured in 1967, and upon the re-establishment of the people of Palestine in their own state on their own land. Of the other Arab countries besides Egypt, some supported Mr. Sadat, but others attacked him violently on the ground that his trip was itself an implicit recognition of the State of Israel and thus a betrayal of the Arab cause.

When Israeli Prime Minister Begin responded on the same occasion, he did not mention — but neither did he retract — the four principles basic, in Israel's opinion, to peace. Foreign Minister Moshe Dayan had stated them in a news conference only a few weeks before (on October 10, 1977), prior to an address he made to the General Assembly of the United Nations. He listed as essential (1) the security of Israel; (2) freedom of navigation in international waterways; (3) the security of main water sources such as the Jordan River sources in the north; and (4) equal rights and full coexistence between Israel and Palestinian Arabs in the Gaza Strip and in Judea and Samaria (the biblical names for the West Bank). What Begin did do was declare that "everything is open to negotiation . . . ," and claim that "there is nothing that can be excluded." He then expressed Israel's readiness to meet with the representatives of Egypt, Jordan, Syria, and Lebanon in a peace conference in Geneva.

Thus President Sadat and Prime Minister Begin parted at the close of this unprecedented and momentous meeting making mutual pledges of "no more war" and "peace and security" for both nations, and promising to work together toward those goals.

The "peace process" which ensued was long and difficult, and the United States became increasingly involved in efforts to help the two sides reach some kind of agreement on their many specific problems. At the invitation of President Carter, President Sadat and Prime Minister Begin met with him at Camp David in September 1978, and new accords were announced, apparently signaling the signing of a peace treaty shortly thereafter. Again, however, there were long delays and many frustrations, as old problems remained and new problems developed.

Finally Mr. Carter went in person to Egypt and Israel; and even then, on the next-to-the-last day of his stay in the Middle East, the matter still appeared impossible to resolve. But on March 13, 1979, as President Carter flew home, it was announced that both President Sadat and Prime Minister Begin had agreed upon all outstanding points and would sign a peace treaty if it were approved by both the Egyptian Parliament and the Israeli Knesset. In the next days such approval was granted, and Sadat and Begin signed the treaty in Washington, D.C., on March 26, 1979.

According to the terms of the treaty Israel is to withdraw in Sinai behind a boundary running from el-Arish on the Mediterranean to Ras Muhammad on the Red Sea; Israel is to have the right of passage in the Suez Canal and the Gulf of Aqabah; and Israel and Egypt together are to try to implement within one year an agreement on Palestinian self-rule.

The Palestinian question is enormously important; the 1979 treaty, it is hoped, is a first step toward its resolution, and toward a broader peace in the Middle East. Certainly the further steps taken toward that larger goal must be planned with particular care if there is indeed to be a lasting peace in the entire region.

II. ITS DILEMMA:
What Is a Just Peace?

In the historic meeting of the Knesset in Jerusalem on November 20, 1977, President Sadat presented a Muslim-Arab view of the situation in Palestine, and Prime Minister Begin presented an Israeli-Jewish view. But in addition to these two views, there are various other perspectives — ones which complicate the problem of establishing a just peace. A discussion of these views follows.

A. THE VIEWS OF CHRISTIAN ARABS

Christian Arabs constitute perhaps a seven percent minority in the Arab world, but nonetheless play an important part in affairs. Among them a small group supports Zionism; another small group thinks that Christians should convert Jews and thereby end the threat of Zionism. But the majority sides with the Muslim Arabs, who feel that they are engaged in a struggle to regain their rightful place in Palestine. (In fact, many of the leaders of the Palestinian resistance movement are Christians, notably George Habash of the Popular Front for the Liberation of Palestine.) Each of these three positions has been interestingly articulated by an important spokesman for it.

Ighnatiyus Mubarak, the Maronite Archbishop of Beirut (the Maronites are an Eastern Christian sect in union with Rome), expresses the opinion of the pro-Zionists well:

> "We Christian Lebanese . . . realize that Zionism is bringing civilization to Palestine and to the entire Middle East. I am very much in favor of Zionism because I have the good of Palestine at heart. If you wish to follow the desires of Moslem Arabs, they want to dominate the country and to cast the Christians out. I tell you frankly that if you oppose Zionism in Palestine it means returning the people to the domination of savagery and the country to the state of anarchy and bribery in which it existed under the Ottoman Sultans. . . . Here is a struggle between civilization and regression. . . . We Christian Lebanese prefer civilization to regression."

The Christian intellectual Adib Nassur wrote a book about Israel's problems called *The Setback and the Error: The Intellectual and Ideological Errors Which Led to the Disaster,* published in Beirut in 1968. He explains the Christians' insistence on Jewish conversion:

> "Israel's problem is . . . the problem of existing and continuing in history contrary to the Divine Purpose of history. . . . The true solution to the problem of the Jews in the world is not to exterminate them, as Hitler did, nor in their assimilation into the nations [in which they live], nor in Zionism. . . . Salvation consists of those who are suffering, because they have . . . accepted Christ. . . . The [Christian] Church is God's new [Chosen] People."

Expressing the majority's opinion is Constantine Zurayq, a professor of history at the American University in Beirut who considers the regaining of Palestine essential and laments the status of the cause:

> "Often have we orated, written and proclaimed that Palestine was our primary cause. But has it really been so? . . . Any division in the Arab ranks takes attention from the Palestine cause, demotes it from its proper primary position to a lowly status, allows the enemy to prepare and mobilize, weakens the Arabs' effort in preparing, and earns for them weakness and loss when fighting breaks out."

B. THE VIEWS OF JEWS IN THE UNITED STATES

Jews in the United States have for the most part been intensely interested in the State of Israel, but most of them do not intend to move there. Proponents of both conservative and radical theologies strongly support declaring the State of Israel the proper homeland of Judaism and the refuge for Jews from lands of oppression, but Jewish adherents of the so-called New Left have criticized the idea. Each of these positions is forcefully expressed in the following paragraphs.

In 1940 conservative rabbi Israel Goldstein wrote eloquently about the importance of Zionism:

> Palestine is the heart of Jewish hope and promise. Zionism is the spiritual dynamic of the Jewish people. It helps to give spiritual content to Jewish life everywhere. Zionism offers the guarantee that when democracy will triumph in

---

Additional Reading on the Positions of the Christian Arabs

Haddad, William W. "Christian Arab Attitudes toward the Arab-Israeli Conflict." *The Muslim World,* 67 (1977), 127-145. This article contains the three quotations given above, and others illustrative of the subject.

Runciman, Steven. *The Historic Role of the Christian Arabs of Palestine.* Harlow, England: Longmans for the University of Essex, 1970. A sympathetic exposition.

the world, Judaism will not melt away under the sun of freedom. It is the supreme expression of the mystic will to live which is the stubborn fact of Jewish history.

A radical Jewish theologian, Richard L. Rubenstein, professor of religion at Florida State University, made a similarly supportive statement at the First International Scholars' Conference on the German Church Struggle and the Holocaust, held in 1970:

> "I have elected to accept what Camus has rightly called the courage of the absurd, the courage to live in a meaningless, purposeless Cosmos rather than believe in a God who inflicts Auschwitz on his people.... After Auschwitz, I am a pagan. To be a pagan means to find once again one's roots as a child of Earth and to see one's own existence as wholly and totally an earthly existence.... Though every single establishment Jewish theologian rejects this position, the Jewish people have given their assent — with their feet. They have gone home."

On the other hand, Joseph L. Blau, professor in the Department of Religion at Columbia University, describes the resistance to Zionism. He observes that the relationship between American Jewry and world Zionism has not been free from tension, and notes a recent development of this tension: the establishment of the so-called New Left in America, a Jewish fragment which is intensely anti-Israel. The position of the New Left is effectively described by Marshall Sklare:

> In the extreme New Left version of the Middle East conflict Israel is regarded as an imperialist nation bent on subverting progressive Arab regimes. In a more mild interpretation Israel is regarded as an ally and tool of American imperialism. Consequently American Jews who support Israel are guilty of

---

Additional Reading on the Positions of the Jews

To find an elaboration of these positions in general and the above quotations in particular, see the following:

Blau, Joseph L. *Judaism in America: From Curiosity to Third Faith.* Chicago: University of Chicago Press, 1976, p. 89.

Goldstein, Israel. *Towards a Solution.* New York: Putnam, 1940, p. 176.

Rubenstein, Richard L. In *The German Church Struggle and the Holocaust.* Ed. Franklin H. Littell and Hubert G. Locke. Detroit: Wayne State University Press, 1974, pp. 262, 267. See also Richard L. Rubenstein, *After Auschwitz: Radical Theology and Contemporary Judaism.* Indianapolis: Bobbs-Merrill, 1966. Cf. Emil L. Fackenheim, *God's Presence in History: Jewish Affirmations and Philosophical Reflections.* New York: New York University Press, 1970. Rubenstein sees the Jew after Auschwitz as the embodiment of endurance even if abandoned by God and man. For a review of the positions of Rubenstein and others, see Jerome Eckstein, "The Holocaust and Jewish Theology," in *Midstream,* 24 (1977), 36-45.

Sklare, Marshall. *America's Jews.* New York: Random House, 1971, p. 221.

supporting American foreign policy. Thus in contrast to the old fear that Jews who support Israel would be regarded as disloyal to America, Jews who support Israel are now being charged with loyalty to America.

C. THE VIEWS OF ROMAN CATHOLICS

The popes, principal articulators of Roman Catholic opinion, have varied greatly in their attitudes toward Palestine. Pope Benedict XV (1914-1922) offered somewhat qualified approval of the plan for a Jewish homeland in Palestine. On the other hand, Pope Pius XI (1922-1939) opposed the plan strongly. And it is surprising to note that Pope Pius XII (1939-1958) knew in detail of the Nazi attempt to exterminate the Jews but did not utter any protest. In apology for this and other similar misjudgments, Pope John XXIII (1958-1963) wrote this penitential prayer shortly before his death on June 3, 1963:

> "We now acknowledge that for many, many centuries blindness has covered our eyes, so that we no longer see the beauty of Thy chosen people and no longer recognize in its face the features of our first-born brother. We acknowledge that the mark of Cain is upon our brow. For centuries Abel lay low in blood and tears because we forgot Thy love. Forgive us the curse that we wrongfully pronounced upon the name of the Jews. Forgive us that we crucified Thee in the flesh for the second time. For we know not what we did. . . ."

Pope Paul VI (1963-1978) considered President Sadat's visit to Israel a great and hopeful event. The Pope said:

> "The head of the Egyptian people today visits — joyfully welcomed — the land of Israel. Does this mean that a 30-year manifold war is concluding? Is peace blossoming again in a painful strategic region of the world? Does this mean that an ultrapolitical concord, polarized by the sovereign worship to a single living God, is beginning?"

He also reiterated the long-standing concern for the Palestinians, describing them as those who had suffered most.

This concern for the Palestinians was reiterated in editorials in the September 1-8 (p. 84) and October 13, 1979 (pp. 185-186) issues of *America*, published by the Jesuits of the United States and Canada. These editorials recalled an important point made at the Rabat Conference of Arab states, held soon after the Arab-Israeli war of June 1967. At that time the Palestine Liberation Organization was recognized as the sole legitimate spokesman for the Palestinian people, but it was also described as a group that helped to precipitate the armed conflict that has pitted Christian against Muslim in Lebanon and destroyed the only truly democratic society in the Arab Middle East. One of the editorials said further:

The P.L.O., moreover, tends toward radicalism in its political thinking, which makes conservative Arab states fearful of a West Bank Palestinian state despite public utterances to the contrary. . . . Besides, to pretend that an independent Palestinian state on the West Bank is economically feasible is most unrealistic.

Nevertheless, the editorial affirmed, it is absolutely necessary for the P.L.O. somehow to be brought into the negotiating process, because in the long run the security of Israel itself in the Middle East will turn on the resolution of the Palestinian problem.

Pope John Paul II (1978-   ) made a similar statement. Although he did not mention the Palestine Liberation Organization by name, he warned in a speech (reported in a dispatch from Rome on November 10, 1980) that any attempt to bring about a partial Middle East settlement by excluding the Palestinians or ignoring the status of Jerusalem could lead to a more serious conflict. He declared that efforts for peace must continue "until a comprehensive peace is achieved, a peace which provides an equitable solution to all aspects of the Middle East crisis, including the Palestine problem and the question of Jerusalem."

D. THE VIEWS OF PROTESTANTS IN THE UNITED STATES

Roy Eckardt, a Protestant theologian and head of the Department of Religion at Lehigh University, and Alice Eckardt, a specialist in Jewish-Christian relations, write of the challenge to the conscience that the Palestinian issue poses:

> A nation either has a right to sovereign existence or it does not. There is no such thing as a partial right to exist. Accordingly, we who believe that Israel does possess the right to exist are compelled at this one crucial point to oppose any Arab denial of that right, even though we find much that is of value in the Arab cause. . . . Together with large numbers of Israelis, we believe that the claims of the Palestinian Arabs must be taken seriously. Many of the arguments advanced for Jewish rights to the land can be presented in behalf of the Palestinians. We

---

Additional Reading on Roman Catholic Pronouncements

For these facts about the Popes and their pronouncements, see the following:

Eckardt, Alice, and Roy Eckardt. *Encounter with Israel: A Challenge to Conscience.* New York: Association Press, 1970, pp. 194, 238, 255.

Keller, Werner. *Diaspora: The Post-Biblical History of the Jews.* New York: Harcourt, Brace and World, 1969, p. ix.

Rubenstein, Richard L. In *The German Church Struggle and the Holocaust.* Ed. Franklin H. Littell and Hubert G. Locke. Detroit: Wayne State University Press, 1974, p. 259.

Associated Press dispatches from Vatican City published on November 21 and December 16, 1977, and a Reuters dispatch from Rome published in the *New York Times* November 11, 1980.

must try our best to understand their anger, frustration, and longings. . . . At the foundation of the affirmation of Israel is the right to life that every people must have if the Jewish people are to share in it. From this foundation arises a specific right created by history, the right of Jews to a certain place once known as Palestine. This, too, is a shared right, shared with Palestinian Arabs.

Additional Reading on Protestant Attitudes Toward Israel

Eckardt, Alice, and Roy Eckardt. *Encounter with Israel: A Challenge to Conscience.* New York: Association Press, 1970, pp. 194, 238, 255.

A recent publication was the *CCI Notebook* of the Christians Concerned for Israel, P.O. Box 2387, Philadelphia, PA 19103. In addition to listing recent relevant books, the *Notebook* made incisive comments about current events affecting Israel. For example (in N.S. No. 1, 11/77), there was an article about the virtual incorporation of Lebanon into the sovereignty of Greater Syria (against Maronite Christian resistance), which closed the ring of the so-called confrontation states (Jordan, Syria, Lebanon) around Israel. This has now become *Honor the Promise,* published by the National Christian Leadership Conference for Israel, Suite 700, 1629 K St. NW, Washington, D.C. 20009.

III. ITS PERSONALITY

A. ITS POLITICAL STRUCTURES

The State of Israel is defined as a parliamentary democracy. The supreme authority is in the Assembly, called the Knesset, one house consisting of 120 members elected for four years. The Knesset elects the president of the state for a term of five years, with re-election possible for one further term. Responsible to the Knesset is the Cabinet, which is headed by the prime minister and which appoints other ministers to oversee such matters as foreign affairs and religious affairs.

There are many political parties, and three principal political blocs. The Labor Alignment combines the Israel Labor Party and the United Workers' Party. The Likud (Union) unites the Herut (Freedom) Movement, the Israel Liberal Party (successor to the General Zionists), and certain other groups. The National Religious Party also unites a number of groups. In addition to the three blocs there are an Independent Liberal Party, a New Communist List, and still other groups. In 1978 the Labor Party, led by Shimon Peres, is the opposition party, while the rightest Likud is in power, with Menachem Begin, its leader, in the office of prime minister.

B. ITS POLITICAL LEADERS, PAST AND PRESENT

1. Past Leaders

David Ben-Gurion. David Ben-Gurion is considered the founding father of the State of Israel. Born in 1886 in Plonsk, near Warsaw (at a time when Poland was a part of Russia), he was named David Gruen, but later gave his last name the Hebrew form of Ben-Gurion. As a young man he joined the Zionist movement, and went to Palestine in 1906. A short time before he went, he wrote: "We take with us [to Palestine] young and healthy arms, the love of work, an eagerness for free and natural lives in the land of our forefathers, and a willingness toward frugality." It was his hope to develop there "a model society based on social, economic and political equality."

In Palestine he became a farmer, then founded a political party and a newspaper; he soon rose to the highest political positions. He was chairman of the Jewish Agency for Palestine from 1934 to 1948, and as such he read Israel's Proclamation of Independence to the National Council in Tel Aviv on May 14, 1948. Then he became the country's first prime minister, in office from 1948 to 1954; he was prime minister again from 1956 to 1963. When he retired from office temporarily in 1954, he joined a kibbutz in the Negev which became his permanent home — Sde Boker (Field of the Rancher), approximately 48 km (30 mi) from Beersheba. Here he studied and wrote, and promoted the Sde Boker Institute of Negev Studies, which researches the problems of the arid lands.

Chaim Weizmann. Chaim Weizmann was the head of the World Zionist Organization and the first president of the State of Israel. He was born in 1874 in Motol (near Minsk) in Russia. This region (in which in the nineteenth century Jews were permitted to live permanently) he later described as one of the "darkest and most remote corners of the Pale of the Settlement." He explained how the 200 Jewish families lived in a particular section of town, separated from the 500 Russian families, "for the sake of comfort, security and company."

His accomplishments were many. He became a chemist of international fame; in fact, during the First World War the British War Office asked him to find a way of producing an essential explosive previously made from a substance imported from Germany. In England he was influential in the considerations which led to the Balfour Declaration in 1917; in 1918 he was welcomed in Jerusalem by Kemal Effendi, the Grand Mufti of Jerusalem, with a traditional saying (*hadith*) of Muhammad: "Our rights are your rights, and your duties our duties"; and in 1919 he signed an agreement with the Emir Faisal in which Jewish settlement in Palestine was approved, provided that an Arab state was set up in the surrounding territories. In the 1920's Weizmann continued to seek understanding with the Arabs. In the 1930's he concentrated on attempts to rescue refugees; he is remembered for explaining to a British inquiry commission that the world was divided into two kinds of places: countries where Jews could not stay, and countries which would not permit them to enter. When he was elected president of the State of Israel he was quite old, and he died in 1952 in the middle of his second term.

Yitzchak Ben-Zvi, Zalman Shazar, Ephraim Katzir. After Weizmann's death the position of president, considered largely honorary, was offered to Albert Einstein, a longtime supporter of the Zionist cause, but he refused it. The succeeding presidents were Yitzchak Ben-Zvi (1952-1963), Zalman Shazar (1963-1973), and Ephraim Katzir (1973-1978). All three, like Weizmann, were natives of Russia. Ben-Zvi was a native of Poltava in the southwest; Shazar was born in Mir, near Minsk; and Katzir, first named Ephraim Katchalski, was born in Kiev in 1916 — but he came to Palestine at the age of six. Both Ben-Zvi and Shazar, like Weizmann, began their political careers in Zionist organizations in Russia.

Katzir was active in the movement for agricultural settlements, and served in the Haganah. He specialized in research in molecular biology, and became an internationally acclaimed scientist; from 1949 to 1973 he was head of the Department of Biophysics at the Weizmann Institute of Science at Rehovot. After his election as president he was quoted as saying: "We have an exceptional opportunity to show the world how to control the monster of technology and to create a model society. If we can do this in the next twenty-five years the whole Zionist effort will have been worthwhile."

Moshe Sharett. Moshe Sharett was prime minister during the two years of Ben-Gurion's temporary retirement (1954-1956). Sharett (originally Shartok) was born in 1894 in the Kherson region of the Ukraine in Russia; he came to Palestine at the age of twelve. The family's first home was in an Arab village in the hills of Samaria, and the boy learned to speak fluent Arabic. Later the family moved to Jaffa and settled in the new Jewish quarter on the sand dunes, which became Tel Aviv.

As a young man Sharett studied law in Constantinople and economics in London. Back in Palestine he became head of the political department of the Jewish Agency, and took a leading part in the diplomatic struggle for independence. In the government of the new State of Israel he served as foreign minister, retaining this position even while he was prime minister. When Ben-Gurion returned as prime minister, Sharett continued for a time as foreign minister, then was succeeded by Golda Meir. He died in 1956.

Levi Eshkol. Born in the Ukraine in 1895, Levi Eshkol came to Palestine from Kiev in 1914. Three years after he left home his father was killed in a Russian pogrom.

Eshkol succeeded Ben-Gurion as prime minister in 1963. On the eve of the Six-Day War in 1967 Eshkol was able to form a government of national unity which for the first time brought together almost all of the political parties — except the Communists — in the face of this great danger. It was also he who sent the message on June 5, 1967, to King Hussein in Amman asking that Jordan stay out of the war. When Hussein did not cooperate, the Israeli forces, fighting back, took the Old City of Jerusalem and the West Bank of the Jordan, as well as the territory in Sinai, the Gaza Strip, and the Golan Heights. Two years later, in 1969, Eshkol died in office.

Golda Meir. Mrs. Golda Meir succeeded Eshkol as prime minister in 1969. Born in Kiev in the Ukraine in 1898, she went to the United States in 1906. After working as a school teacher in Milwaukee, she came to Palestine in 1921, and settled in a cooperative village as an agricultural worker. She served on the executive committee of the Histadrut, and became head of its political department, then head of the political department of the Jewish Agency.

On May 10, 1948, four days before the proclamation of the new State of Israel, she went on a hazardous mission across the border, dressed in the black robes and veil of an Arab woman. She met secretly with King Abdullah (grandfather of King Hussein) and tried (unsuccessfully) to persuade him not to send in the Arab Legion when the British withdrew. In 1948, with the establishment of the State of Israel, she was appointed the first Israeli ambassador to the Soviet Union. When she arrived in Moscow and went on the first Rosh Hashanah to the Great Synagogue, there was a joyous demonstration by tens of thousands of Soviet Jews, who saw her as the embodiment of the new Jewish sovereignty in Palestine.

In 1949 she was elected to the First Knesset and appointed minister of labor, and from 1956 to 1966 was foreign minister. Then she was secretary-general of the Israel Workers' Party, then known as the Mapai; next she held the same position in the new Israel Labor Party. After two years she retired because of increasing age, deteriorating health, and weariness, but within a year she returned to the political world with renewed energy. After the death of Eshkol in 1969, in fact, she became prime minister, and only resigned in 1974 after the government was criticized for its handling of the Yom Kippur War in 1973.

She was highly respected even after her resignation. When President Sadat visited in November 1977 she was still one of the country's most prominent figures, and was most warmly greeted by Mr. Sadat, who said: "I have waited a long time for this."

Meir was truly dedicated to the Jewish cause. Although described as a lifelong secular Jew, in 1970 she said, "In the twentieth century we shall not throw away the prayer shawl and the phylacteries," and in 1972 she declared that there is no difference between Jewish religion and Jewish nationhood: "An American may be an Anglican-American or a Buddhist-American, but I have never seen an Anglican-Jew or a Buddhist-Jew." Looking back upon her life, she has recalled her childhood days in Kiev when the Jews boarded up the doors and windows of their homes to protect themselves against marauding Ukrainian peasants, and watched mounted Cossacks ride through the streets and set their houses afire. About her life's work she has said: "If there is any logical explanation necessary to the direction which my life has taken, maybe this is the explanation: the desire and determination to save Jewish children, four or five years old, from a similar scene, from a similar experience."

Yitzchak Rabin. Yitzchak Rabin succeeded Golda Meir in 1974. Up until this time Israel's top leaders had been part of the generation of pioneer settlers in the land, but Rabin was a Sabra, a native Israeli, born in Jerusalem in 1922.

An impressive military and political career preceded his rule as prime minister. When the Second World War broke out, the Haganah encouraged volunteers to enlist in the British Army to fight Nazi Germany, and in 1941 the British authorized the formation in Palestine of Palmah (Plugot Mahatz) commando companies, which fought against the Vichy French on the Syrian and Lebanese borders. Rabin joined the Palmah when it was founded, and fought in Syria. After the war he was also active in the underground movement against the British mandatory government. In the War of Independence in 1948 he commanded a brigade, and was prominent in the fight for Jerusalem. As chief of staff at the time of the Six-Day War in 1967, he played a major role in planning the campaign. Then in 1968 he became the ambassador to the United States, serving in that post until 1973; in 1974 he became prime minister, holding office until 1977.

2. Present Leaders

Yitzchak Navon. In 1978, with the expiration of Ephraim Katzir's presidential term approaching, Prime Minister Begin nominated the nuclear physicist Yitzchak Chavet for the position. Chavet, born in Cairo of Syrian-Jewish parentage, was a member of the Sephardic-Oriental community — one reason that Begin nominated him, because one of his goals was to place more Sephardim in prominent positions. (The Sephardim have actually come to constitute the majority in Israel, but they still lag behind the Ashkenazim, or European Jews, in education and in representation in high public positions.)

The Knesset, however, elected a different man — Yitzchak Navon. Born in Jerusalem fifty-seven years before, he was secretary to David Ben-Gurion for eleven years, and was a member of the Labor Party and an officeholder in the previous Labor government. He, like Chavet, was in fact a member of the Sephardic-Oriental community. When he was sworn in for a five-year term on May 29, 1978, he thus became Israel's first president from the Sephardic-Oriental community, as well as its first native president. Among his objectives as president, he has said, is the mending of relations with Israel's 500,000 Arabs, and he has called for negotiations with any Palestinian organization that will recognize Israel.

Menachem Begin. In 1980 Menachem Begin is Israel's prime minister, having succeeded Yitzchak Rabin in this position early in 1977. Begin was born on August 13, 1913, in Brest-Litovsk in Poland, and was later a student of law at Warsaw University. As a young man he became politically involved. In 1925 a Russian Jew named Vladimir Jabotinsky founded the so-called Revisionist movement, which split from the World Zionist Organization in 1935, calling for more militant dealings with the British and for the establishment of a Jewish state on both sides of the Jordan River. The youth group of the movement was called Betar (named after Brit Trumpeldor, who died in 1920 in the defense of the frontier settlement in Tel Hai in Palestine). Already as a secondary-school student in Brest-Litovsk, Begin was a militant member of Betar; after he studied law he became one of the finest orators of the movement.

When Jabotinsky died in 1940, Begin voluntarily submitted to arrest by the Soviet authorities in the Lithuanian city of Vilna, and was in a Soviet concentration camp until 1941. He said at the time: "If we cannot fight for our country [Israel], then we shall suffer for it." When he was released at the end of 1941, he went to Palestine. There he joined the Irgun Zvai Leumi (National Military Organization), the underground movement active in the days of the British mandatory government. Already in 1937 the Jewish Haganah's attempts to repel Arab attacks and to rescue Jewish refugees had seemed insufficient to some of Jabotinsky's disciples in the Revisionist movement, and they had left the Haganah and formed this organization.

The first commander of the Irgun was David Raziel, killed on a mission in Iraq; in 1943 Begin became the second commander. In 1946 the Irgun blew up part of the King David Hotel in Jerusalem, which was used by the British as headquarters; in 1948 they fought in the Palestinian village of Deir Vassin, where 200 Arab inhabitants were killed. (The group may not have been as committed to violence as these incidents suggest: in both cases, it is said, advance warnings of the attacks were ignored.) In June 1948, when the United Nations had proclaimed a truce in Arab-Israeli fighting and had forbidden the import of arms into the area, Begin nonetheless brought a ship, the *Altadena,* into Tel Aviv with a cargo of weapons intended for the Irgun. But at Ben-Gurion's orders the ship was fired upon; it sank and the guns were lost.

After this clash with Ben-Gurion, Begin dissolved the Irgun and founded in 1948 a political party called the Herut (Freedom) Party, which opposed the Labor-dominated coalition governments of the time. He was also elected to the Knesset. In 1965 the Herut joined with the Israel Liberal Party to form the Gahal (a word meaning "charcoal," but also the acronym of Gush Herut Liberalim), and then in 1973 joined with yet other groups to make the present Likud Party, which chose Begin as its leader. After the resignation of Prime

Minister Rabin on April 8, 1977, general elections were held on May 17. The outcome: the Likud Party became the largest group in the Ninth Knesset, and Begin became prime minister. In 1980 Begin is holding the position of defense minister as well.

Shimon Peres. Shimon Peres (formerly Persky) is the leader of Israel's opposition Labor Party. He was born in 1923 in the town of Wolozyn in what was then a part of Poland and is now a part of the U.S.S.R. Settling in Palestine in 1934, he joined the Haganah, and was one of a group of students who founded Alumot, a kibbutz in eastern Lower Galilee. He served in the Ministry of Defense from 1948 to 1959, and was elected to the Knesset in 1959. He was also active in the Mapai (Israel Workers' Party), and in the formation of the new Israel Labor Party in 1967. In 1970 he was made the minister of transportation and communication; in 1974 he became defense minister.

In November 1980, the Labor Party — in anticipation of national elections to be held no later than November 1981 — drafted the defense and foreign affairs planks of its platform. It called for the establishment of a single Jordanian-Palestinian state within the boundaries of the present nation of Jordan east of the Jordan River, as well as in the densely inhabited parts of the West Bank and the Gaza Strip. Under a peace treaty, Israel would evacuate these latter two areas, giving the newly formed state a Palestinian majority. On November 11, 1980, the *San Francisco Chronicle* (quoting from a dispatch sent from Tel Aviv to the *New York Times*) cited Shimon Peres as endorsing this position. At the same time Prime Minister Begin's Herut Party was quoted as warning of "a national catastrophe" if the Labor Party wins the election; and Interior Minister Yosef Burg, leader of the influential National Religious Party, whose support would be needed by either the Herut or the Labor Party in order to form a government, said his party would not join any coalition committed to the Labor Party proposal.

Moshe Dayan. Moshe Dayan became minister for foreign affairs in 1977. He is a first-generation Sabra, the second child born (in 1915) in Degania, the first kibbutz in the land. In 1921, when he was six, his parents Shmuel and Dvora Dayan moved to the Jezreel Valley to join in founding Nahalah, the first moshav.

His military career, which spanned many years, was interesting and varied. He fought in the Allied invasion of Syria in 1941, during which he lost his left eye. In 1956, when Egyptian President Nasser announced the nationalization of the Suez Canal, and Great Britain and France bombed Port Said and landed troops in the Canal Zone, Dayan was chief of staff and commander of the Israeli forces in the Sinai campaign. At the time of the Six-Day War of 1967 he was defense minister — and principal character in an interesting incident. Mordecai

Gur (in 1977 the Israeli chief of staff) was then in command of the brigade of paratrooper reservists which took the Old City of Jerusalem. When Colonel Gur reached the Temple area, he hung an Israeli flag from the top of the Western Wall. When General Dayan came, although not himself a praying Jew, he scribbled a prayer on a slip of paper and put it in a crack in the wall, as pious pilgrims have done through the ages. The prayer read: "May peace come to the Jewish people."

After the war Dayan was responsible for the administration of the territories which had been occupied by the Israeli army. On June 29 Dayan changed the administration of the Old City of Jerusalem from military rule to civilian rule, and despite the apprehensive hesitation of the mayor, he insisted that the barriers between East and West Jerusalem be taken down immediately. Thus, for the first time since 1948, Arabs and Jews move freely between East and West Jerusalem.

In 1980 Dayan is no longer foreign minister, but still a member of the Knesset. It is commonly said that it would be difficult to think of the government without him.

Yitzchak Shamir. In 1980 Yitzchak Shamir is the minister for foreign affairs. He was born in Poland in 1915, and, like Menachem Begin, joined the Betar at an early age. In 1935 he emigrated to Israel, and there, again like Begin, he was with the Irgun Zvai Leumi (National Military Organization). After a split in that organization (in 1937), he joined the Lohamei Herut Israel (Israel Freedom Fighters) in 1940-41, and continued with it until the establishment of the State of Israel. Following the murder of Yair Stern (in 1942), Shamir reorganized the Lohamei Herut Israel and coordinated its operational activities. He was twice arrested by the British Mandate Authority, and twice he escaped from the country. In 1948 he returned to Israel, but kept out of the public eye until 1955. In 1970 he joined the Herut (Freedom) Party, and was elected to the Knesset in 1973. He attained his current position after membership in both the defense and the foreign affairs departments.

Yosef Burg. In 1980 Yosef Burg is interior minister and head of the National Religious Party. He was born in Dresden, Germany, in 1909. He received his doctorate from the University of Berlin, and was also ordained as a rabbi in Berlin. In 1939 he settled in Israel, but also spent time in Geneva working for the Youth Aliyah (an organization that endeavored to rescue children and young people from hardship and persecution and give them care and education in Israel). He also spent time in Paris aiding survivors of the Holocaust. A member of the Knesset since 1949, he has held various official positions, including those of minister of health and minister of social welfare. In 1970 he became minister of the interior.

C. ITS WORKING WORLD

Next to the government itself, the country's labor union, the General Federation of Israel Labor (usually known as the Histadrut, which is Hebrew for "organization"), is considered the most powerful body in the country. When it was founded in 1920 it had 5,000 members; now it has approximately one and one-quarter million members embracing an estimated 70 percent of the earning population and including 89,000 Arabs and Druzes. More than 300,000 housewives are also members. The federation has a health organization called Kupat Holim, which serves two out of every three Israelis and operates 15 hospitals, 12 convalescent homes, and 1,000 clinics. In addition, the federation conducts orientation courses for newcomers, publishes two daily newspapers, and sponsors Israel's largest athletic organization, Hapoel.

Affiliated with the Histadrut through its Agricultural Center are the majority of cooperative farming settlements that have become common in Israel. Cooperative farming, in fact, has become a way of life for many in Israel. The first experiment in such collective work on the land was in 1909 at Degania, a settlement founded just south of the Sea of Galilee. From this experiment has developed the kibbutz, a type of collective farming establishment which is unique to Israel. In the kibbutz there is no individual ownership of home or land; the only private property is personal belongings. The individual works for the group under the direction of the works committee, while the group takes care of the individual's needs.

Similar to the kibbutz is the moshav, a slightly different kind of cooperative settlement first developed in 1921, when a number of people broke away from Degania. In the moshav, as in the kibbutz, the land belongs to the Jewish

---

Additional Reading on Leaders of Israel

Ben-Gurion, David. *Israel: A Personal History.* New York: Funk and Wagnalls, 1971.
_____. *Memoirs.* Ed. Thomas R. Branstein. New York: World Publishing, 1970.
Comay, Joan. *Who's Who in Jewish History From the Old Testament to the Present.* New York: McKay, 1974. Describes individuals from Bar-Kochba to Menachem Beigin (note spellings). With illustrations.
Dayan, Moshe. *Living with the Bible.* London: Weidenfeld and Nicolson, 1978.
Elon, Amos. *The Israelis: Founders and Sons.* New York: A Bantam Book by arrangement with Holt, Rinehart and Winston, 1972. Recent history told largely through descriptions of the persons who made it.
Meir, Golda. *My Life.* New York: Putnam, 1975.
Who's Who in Israel. Rev. periodically. Tel Aviv: Mamut Ltd.

Though moshavs like this one in Upper Galilee share many characteristics with the kibbutz, a moshav is a cooperative settlement, whereas a kibbutz is a collective settlement.

The fertile lands around the beautiful Sea of Galilee provide attractive locations for the collective agricultural settlements known as kibbutzim.

National Fund, and the buying of supplies and the marketing of products are done cooperatively. The individual member of a moshav, however, lives in a private family house and farms a personally controlled plot of land.

Additional Reading on the Kibbutz

Leon, Dan. *The Kibbutz: A New Way of Life.* Oxford: Pergamon Press, 1969.
Spiro, Melford E. *Kibbutz: Venture in Utopia.* New York: Schocken Books, 1963.
Two books describing the kibbutz as a new social and economic experiment.

In a street in Beersheba, a single bicycle contrasts vividly with the traditional dress of the men standing near it. In partiarchal times Abraham, Isaac, and Jacob lived here. Today it is a major center in the Negev, important to irrigation projects in this arid region.

D. ITS PEOPLE

In 1972 the total population of the State of Israel was 3,200,500. The religious communities distinguishing it are the Jewish, Karaite, Samaritan, Muslim, Christian, Druze, and Bahai.

1. The Jews

The great majority of the population of Israel is Jewish: the Jews numbered 2,723,600 in 1972. Of these, about 48 percent are persons who were born in Israel. They are commonly called *Sabras,* which is the Arabic term for the fruit of the cactus plant. It is said that this was once the most popular indigenous fruit, and parents fondly called their children their "little sabras." Later it was suggested that the native Israeli be called a Sabra, because he is often characterized as having a tough exterior but a kind heart, and the fruit is tough and prickly on the outside but soft and sweet inside. This explanation of the term is now common.

When the Law of Return was passed in 1950, which assured the right of every Jew — wherever he might come from — to live in Israel as a citizen, the question was raised, Who is a Jew? The question is surprisingly difficult to answer; there is, in fact, no legal definition. The most widely accepted answer is simply that a Jew is a person born of a Jewish mother or converted to Judaism. Because of an amendment of the Law of Return in 1970, however, Israeli nationality is also granted to the spouse of any immigrant Jew. According to this broad definition of Jewishness, which says little about religious and/or philosophical convictions, a Jew may be anyone from an Orthodox Jew of Mea Shearim (a Jerusalem suburb where the men grow beards and side-curls and wear fur-brimmed hats) to a secularist, whose devotion is simply to the land and/or to the social order the secularists are trying to establish.

The Jewish faith is easier to define: it is based upon the Talmud (the Mishnah and Gemara) and the Hebrew Bible (the Torah — the first five books of the Bible; the Prophets — Joshua through II Kings; and the Writings — the remaining books in the Old Testament). The Talmud is a vast repository of religious and ethical teachings, jurisprudence, and folklore, the complete text of which constitutes more than thirty large volumes. Additional to it are still more rabbinical materials known as the Midrash (meaning "explanation," this being of two kinds — Halakah, or rules, and Haggadah, or stories). The Talmud and the Midrash could be the object of lifelong study, because there is much in both that is difficult to grasp, yet in them are also such immediately understandable sayings as these:

> What is hateful to you, never do to a fellow person: that is the whole Law — all the rest is commentary.
> If you add to the truth, you subtract from it.
> The Torah begins with acts of loving and ends with kindness; it begins with God clothing Adam and Eve, and ends with God burying Moses.... The beginning and end of the Torah is performing acts of loving-kindness.
> When a child is born, all rejoice; when someone dies, all weep. We should do the opposite. For no one can tell what trials and travails await a newborn child; but when a mortal dies in peace, we should rejoice, for he has completed a long journey, and there is no greater boon than to leave this world with the imperishable crown of a good name.

In Judaism in Israel the Chief Rabbinate is the supreme religious authority. This body includes two Chief Rabbis — one Ashkenazi (German) and one Sephardi (Hispano-Portuguese) — and the Supreme Rabbinical Council. Associated with it are the regional rabbinical courts. There are also almost 6,000 synagogues, and almost 400 officially appointed rabbis.

The weekly holy day is the Sabbath, reckoned from sunset Friday to sunset Saturday. The main festivals of the religious year are numerous: they include the Passover and the Feast of Unleavened Bread, which occurs from the fourteenth to the twenty-first in the first month Nisan (Mar./Apr.); Weeks, or Pentecost, occurring fifty days later in the third month Sivan (May/June); Rosh Hashanah, or New Year's Day, which is the first day of the seventh month Tishri (Sept./Oct.); Yom Kippur, the Day of Atonement, which falls on the tenth day of the seventh month; Sukkot, or Booths, a week-long celebration beginning on the fifteenth day of the seventh month, climaxed by the Simhat Torah, or "Joy of the Law" festival; Hanukkah ("dedication"), or Lights, the commemoration of the rededication of the Temple under Judas Maccabeus, which occurs on the twenty-fifth day of the ninth month Kislev (Nov./Dec.); and Purim ("lots"), the celebration of the deliverance of the Jews from Haman by Esther and Mordecai, which occurs on the fourteenth day of the twelfth month Adar (Feb./Mar.).

2. *The Karaites*

The Karaites are a Jewish sect founded by Anan ben David in Baghdad in 760 C.E., and later led by him to Jerusalem. Now living chiefly in or near Ramla, the Karaites, who number about 10,000, have nine synagogues. They claim to restore primitive Judaism by repudiating the oral tradition of the rabbis and accepting only the literal law of the Bible. They quote the saying of Anan in support of their belief system: "Search well in the Torah, and do not rely on my opinion."

Additional Reading on Jewish Literature and Observances

To learn more about the Talmud, see: Cohen, A. *Everyman's Talmud*. New York: Dutton, 1949. A summary of the Talmud's teachings about God; human beings; physical, moral, domestic, and social life; folklore and jurisprudence; and the hereafter.

To learn more about the festivals and fasts, see the series published by the Jewish Publication Society of America (Philadelphia): Emily Solis-Cohen, *Hanukkah, The Feast of Lights* (1937); Abraham E. Millgram, *Sabbath, The Day of Delight* (1944); Philip Goodman, *The Purim Anthology* (1949), *The Passover Anthology* (1961), *The Yom Kippur Anthology* (1971), *The Sukkot and Simhat Torah Anthology* (1973). These volumes amplify their descriptions of the various occasions with materials from the Bible and rabbinical sources as well as from Jewish prose, poetry, prayers, folklore, art, and music. They also describe the observances in various lands.

Additional Reading on the Karaites

Birnbaum, Philip. *Karaite Studies*. New York: Hermon Press, 1971. A collection in one volume of several scholarly studies of the sect's origins and teachings.

Unsdorfer, J. *The Karaite Day of Atonement Liturgy*. Leeds University Oriental Society, Monograph Series 2, 1963. Delineates the distinctive ideas of the Karaites about Yom Kippur, with translations of some of the texts and prayers they use in its observance.

At Nablus, in the heart of ancient Samaria, three Samaritan priests proudly display the Samaritan scriptures. Consisting only of the Pentateuch, the text is reputedly as old as the sect itself. Today a remnant of this sect prizes its scriptures and continues its distinctive practices.

3. The Samaritans

The Samaritans are now only a remnant of the ancient Samaritan people: there are only about 250 in Nablus and about 230 in Holon, near Tel Aviv. They recognize only the Torah (i.e., the first five books of the Bible). The annual Passover sacrifice they conduct on Mount Gerizim, which they regard as their sacred mountain.

Additional Reading on the Samaritans

Bowman, John. *The Samaritan Problem*. Pittsburgh: Pickwick Press, 1975. This study estimates that Samaritanism developed in the early fourth century B.C.E. at the earliest, and discusses the Samaritans' relationships with other sectarian groups, including the people of Qumran.

Coggins, R. J. *Samaritans and Jews*. Atlanta: John Knox Press, 1975. This reconsideration of the origins of Samaritanism concludes that the formative period was the last three centuries B.C.E.

Macdonald, John. *The Samaritan Day of Atonement Liturgy*. Leeds University Oriental Society, Monograph Series 3, 1963. Translations of hymns and prayers used by the Samaritans on Yom Kippur, with an analysis of what they reveal of "a puzzled anxiety and perplexity that 'the true Israel' should be subjected for so long to persecution and decline."

_____. *The Theology of the Samaritans*. London: SCM Press, 1964. Delineates their basic ideas about God and the world, about Moses and the Taheb, who is expected to bring victory to the elect in the time of the Second Kingdom.

4. The Muslims

In the State of Israel in 1972 there were 476,900 non-Jews; of these, 358,600 were Arabs. In Jerusalem about 25 percent of the population is Arab. The majority of these Arabs are Muslims, followers of the teachings of the prophet Muhammad.

The teachings of Muhammad are found in the Koran, a book of 114 surahs, or chapters, compiled after Muhammad's death and, after the opening chapter, generally arranged according to length, from the longest to the shortest chapter. Originally written in Arabic, the Koran was first translated into a western language — medieval Latin — by an English scholar in the twelfth century; since that time there have been many more translations. In a modern translation the opening surah reads:

> In the Name of God, the Merciful, the Compassionate.
> Praise belongs to God, the Lord of all Being,
> the All-merciful, the All-compassionate,
>   the Master of the Day of Doom.
> Thee only we serve; to Thee alone we pray for succour.
>   Guide us in the straight path,
> the path of those whom Thou hast blessed,
> not of those against whom Thou art wrathful,
>   nor of those who are astray.

In addition to communicating the revelations which he himself received, in the Koran Muhammad makes many references to biblical persons and events — especially to Abraham and Moses, and also to Jesus.

The religious duties of a Muslim, referred to as the five pillars of faith, are the following: (1) recital of the profession of faith: "There is no god but Allah, and Muhammad is the apostle of Allah"; (2) offering prayers toward Mecca at the muezzin's call five times a day; (3) almsgiving; (4) fasting; (5) pilgrimage, if possible, to Mecca.

The great fast (*sawm*) is that of the month of Ramadan, the ninth month of the lunar year. Abstinence from food and drink is required every day of this month from the time in the morning when "a white thread can be distinguished from a black thread" until sunset. This month is named, and its significance stated, in Surah 2:181:

> ...the month of Ramadan, wherein the Quran
> was sent down as a guidance to all men
>   and as evidences of the guidance
> and as a criterion of right and wrong.
> So whoever of you is then at home
> let him fast the month.

And whoever of you is sick or on a journey
let him fast the same number of other days.

At the end of the Fast of Ramadan there is a Feast of the Breaking of the Fast
(Id al-Fitr) — also known as the Minor Feast — when there is general rejoicing.

The ceremonies of the pilgrimage (*hajj*) to Mecca are held during the first
ten days of the twelfth month (called Dhu al-Hijjah, or Master of the
Pilgrimage), and are climaxed by the sacrifice of a sheep by each pilgrim in the
Valley of Mina, near Mecca. This sacrificial practice has been adopted by the rest
of the Muslim world; it is now known as the Id al-Adha, the Feast of the
Sacrifice, or Id al-Kabir, the Great Feast. It commemorates Abraham's
willingness to sacrifice his son (believed to have been Ishmael rather than Isaac)
and the substitution of a sheep (a ram in Gen. 22:13) for the youth.

*A painting commemorating Muhammad's pilgrimage marks the Door of a Hajji (Muhammad)
in Aqahat et-Takiyeh in the Old City of Jerusalem. Today the Five Pillars of Islam — the
practical duties of a follower of Muhammad — include symbolically repeating this pilgrimage.*

In Palestine there is also a pilgrimage which occurs at the same time as the Good Friday services of the Eastern churches. The destination is the shrine of Nebi Musa (the Prophet Moses), which is in the Wilderness of Judea west of the northwestern corner of the Dead Sea. According to Deuteronomy 34:6 Moses' burial-place is unknown, though in 1269 the Mamluk Sultan Baibars built a mosque at the place thought to be the prophet's burial-place. On the pilgrim route between Jerusalem and the Dead Sea, it is a spot from which the pilgrims could see Mount Nebo. Many now actually think that the mosque marks Moses' grave.

In Israel the highest officials of Islam are the four Kadis of four local Sharia Courts. There are about 90 mosques, and more than 200 Muslim clergymen, who are paid by the state.

5. The Druzes
The Druzes are an offshoot of the Muslims, yet are not recognized by orthodox Muslims. They accepted the claim of al-Hakim, the sixth Fatimid caliph of Egypt (996-1021 C.E.), that he was an incarnation of God. First mentioned by

---

Additional Reading on Islam

al Faruqi, Isma'il Ragi A. *On Arabism: 'Urubah and Religion*. Amsterdam: Djambatan, 1962. A book about the fundamental ideas of Arabism, and about Islam as the highest expression of it.

Arberry, Arthur J. *The Koran Interpreted*. 2 vols. London: George Allen and Unwin, 1955. The translation from the Koran used above is from this book.

Cragg, Kenneth. *The Event of the Qur'an: Islam in Its Scriptures*. London: George Allen and Unwin, 1971. The goal of study, says the author, is "an open country of relationship."

Faris, Nabih Amin, ed. *The Arab Heritage*. Princeton: Princeton University Press, 1944. Articles by various contributors on various subjects, including Arabic poetry and science and Islamic art.

Geiger, Abraham. *Judaism and Islam,* with Prolegomenon by Moshe Pearlman. New York: Ktav Publishing House, 1970. Explores the passages in the Koran about biblical subjects and persons.

Hitti, Philip K. *Islam: A Way of Life*. Minneapolis: University of Minnesota Press, 1970. Islam seen as more than a religion — as a culture, a state.

Nomani, Mohammad Manzoor. *The Quran — and You*. Lucknow: al-Furqan Book Depot, 1971. The Quran (Koran) is seen not only as the sacred book of the Muslims but also as a book of guidance for humankind. The material is arranged under topic headings such as "The Divine Attributes," "Submission to Divine Guidance," and "The Love and Service of Humanity."

For details on Islam and the Arabs, see:

The Encyclopaedia of Islam. Rev. ed. Leiden: E. J. Brill, 1960ff. A multi-volume work.

Ronart, Stephen, and Nandy Ronart. *Concise Encyclopaedia of Arabic Civilization*. Amsterdam: Djambatan, 1959. A single volume work.

For current topics, see:

The Muslim World: A Journal Devoted to the Study of Islam and of Christian-Muslim Relationship in Past and Present. Published by The Duncan Black Macdonald Center at The Hartford Seminary Foundation, 55 Elizabeth St., Hartford, Conn. 06105.

name by Benjamin of Tudela when he visited Palestine in 1169 C.E., they are now living in Syria, Lebanon, and Israel, where approximately 38,000 of them live in the town of Shefaram and in eighteen villages in Galilee and on Mount Carmel.

The Druzes call themselves Muwahhidin (Unitarians), believing that there is only one ineffable God, but that he has made himself known by successive incarnations, the final and most perfect being al-Hakim. They also believe in a series of seven prophets: Adam, Noah, Abraham, Moses, Jesus, Muhammad, and a certain Muhammad ibn-Ismail. Their doctrines include a belief in predestination and in the transmigration of souls. Largely hidden from the outside world, their practices include an annual pilgrimage on April 25 to the tomb of Shueib (Shueib they identify as Jethro, the father-in-law of Moses), near the Horns of Hattin in Galilee.

Their recent history includes two noteworthy events: in the War of Independence in 1948 many Druzes fought with the Jewish forces against the Arabs; in 1956 the Israeli Knesset granted the Druzes the status of an autonomous religious community.

6. The Christians

Christians in Israel are mainly Arabs; in 1972 they numbered 79,600. They are divided into thirty denominations and four main groups: (1) Orthodox (Greek, Romanian, Russian); (2) Catholic (Roman, Greek, Maronite, Syrian, Armenian, Chaldean); (3) Monophysite (Armenian, Coptic, Syrian Jacobite, Ethiopian); and (4) Protestant (Anglican, Baptist, Lutheran, Mennonite, Presbyterian, and others). The Greek Orthodox, Latin, and Armenian patriarchs live in Jerusalem, as do the archbishops and bishops of the Anglican, Greek Catholic, Coptic, Ethiopian, and Syrian churches. More than 12,000 Christian laymen live in this city as well; there are also relatively large Christian populations in Bethlehem and Nazareth.

Frequent pilgrimages are a sign of Christian devotion in the Holy Land: thus many of the faithful travel to Bethlehem at Christmas; to the Jordan River, where the place called Mahadet Hajlah or el-Maghtas (the Place of Immersion) is believed to be the place where Jesus was baptized; down the slope of the Mount of Olives on Palm Sunday; along the Via Dolorosa on Good Friday; to the Church of the Holy Sepulcher for the Holy Fire ceremony on the Saturday before Easter; perhaps to the Garden Tomb on Easter; and to the Chapel of the

---

Additional Reading on the Druzes

Hitti, Philip K. *The Origins of the Druze People and Religion.* New York: Columbia University Press, 1928. Also contains excerpts from their little-known sacred writings.

The Jordan River provides the symbolic setting for a Greek Orthodox service of baptism. This area, traditionally thought to be the place where Jesus was baptized, is near a ford in the lower Jordan and close to a monastery named for St. John the Baptist.

Ascension in the Arab village of Kafr et-Tur on the southern summit of the Mount of Olives.

Additional Reading on Arab Christian Observances

Foley, Rolla. *Song of the Arab*. New York: Macmillan, 1953. A description of the religious ceremonies, shrines, and folk music of the Christian Arabs in the Holy Land.

7. *The Bahais*

Two men developed the religion known as Bahaism. The first, Mirza Ali
Muhammad, was born in 1819 at Shiraz in Iran and martyred in 1850 in Tabriz.
A descendant of the prophet Muhammad, he was known as the Bab, or "Gate,"
the forerunner of the movement. The second, Mirza Husayn Ali, who was born
in Iran in 1817 and died in the Holy Land in 1892, was an ardent follower of the
Bab. He became known as Baha'u'llah (the Splendor of God), considered the
long-expected Educator and Teacher of all peoples. Following his teachings,
modern Bahais emphasize the unity of humankind, the common foundation of
all forms of religion, and the ideals of universal peace and human brotherhood
and sisterhood.

Baha'u'llah spent most of the last twenty-four years of his life in a prison in
Acre; the house where he lived when he was released in 1892 and his tomb are
still to be seen 1.6 km (1 mi) north of Acre. The World Center of the Faith is on
the slope of the mountainside in Haifa; there, in a terraced Persian garden, is the
Bahai Shrine, with its golden dome, and a museum and archive building
modeled after the Greek Parthenon.

*The world center of the Bahai faith, at Haifa, is comprised of this elegant shrine and an archive
center. Set in an extensive, beautifully manicured garden, it is halfway up the slope of the Carmel
ridge on which Haifa is built.*

E. ITS LANGUAGES

The official languages in the State of Israel are Hebrew, Arabic, and English. Both Hebrew and Arabic are Semitic languages; both are written from right to left, and each has its own script far different from Latin characters. In Jewish schools the language of instruction is Hebrew; Arabic is an optional language. In Arab schools the language of instruction is Arabic, but Hebrew is also taught from the third grade onward.

Whereas Arabic is the native language of the Arabs, Hebrew is not necessarily the native language of all of the Jews: the Jewish immigrants, having come from many lands, have brought with them many languages. For this reason Theodor Herzl (the founder of Zionism) thought that in a Jewish state there would be many official languages, and did not work at reviving the Hebrew. It was Ben Yehuda, who arrived from Lithuania in 1880, who did most to stimulate the revival of the ancient language and make it the common language of all of the Jews in the land.

At the time he arrived, the Jews in Jerusalem were divided into almost totally separated communities which spoke Yiddish, Ladino, and Arabic. Ben Yehuda, however, insisted on their speaking nothing but Hebrew, working tirelessly to make it usable as a modern language. This was not easy, because until then Hebrew had survived only as a language of the Scriptures, a language of prayer and study — but Ben Yehuda and his successors accomplished the task. When they failed to find a needed word in the Bible, they turned to rabbinical literature and other Semitic languages such as Aramaic and Arabic and, as a last resort, borrowed from European languages.

Ben Yehuda's diligence was quickly rewarded. Already in 1888 the first village school adopted Hebrew as the language of instruction in secular subjects. And in 1904 a Hebrew Language Council was formed, which was granted official status in 1953 as the Academy of Hebrew Language.

F. ITS CALENDAR

All three major faiths in Israel — Jewish, Muslim, and Christian — have a seven-day week. The Hebrew and Arabic languages do not have special names

---

Additional Reading on Bahaism

Esslemont, J. E. *Baha'u'llah and the New Era*. Wilmette, Illinois: Baha'i Publishing Trust, 1970. One of the most widely used introductions to the Bahai faith, published in fifty-eight translations.

Gaver, Jessyca Russell. *The Baha'i Faith: Dawn of a New Day*. New York: Hawthorn Books, 1967. Describes the World Center of the Faith in Haifa and the International Archives, the latter open only to Bahai pilgrims.

for the days of the week, such as Sunday, Monday, Tuesday, etc. (designations developed from the names of the Teutonic gods); instead the days are referred to by number. Using our names, the holy day in the week is Friday for the Muslims, Saturday (called the Sabbath) for the Jews, and Sunday for the Christians. For the Jews the day is reckoned from sunset to sunset; therefore the Sabbath runs from dusk to dusk, and stores and public offices close early on Friday afternoon. The working week begins again on Sunday, simply called "the first day." For Muslims the week begins on Saturday, following the holy day on Friday.

For both Jews and Muslims the beginning of the month is marked by the appearance of the new moon. The Jewish year consists of twelve lunar months, but is kept in step with the solar year by the addition of an extra month seven times in every nineteen years. The Muslim year also has twelve lunar months, but has no provision for a leap year or for the insertion of extra months; therefore a given month gradually shifts position in the calendar, progressing slowly through each season of the solar year. The twelve months of the Christian year, making up a total of 365 days, are not determined by the phases of the moon; this year is harmonized with the solar year by the inclusion of a leap year every fourth year. Two forms of the Christian calendar are used in the Holy Land: the Gregorian calendar, which is generally used in Western countries, and used in Palestine by the Roman Catholic and Protestant churches; and the older Julian calendar, which is used by the Eastern churches such as the Greek Orthodox, Armenian, and Jacobite. In the Julian calendar Easter, Christmas, and New Year's Day are thirteen days later than in the Gregorian calendar.

The three major faiths all determine dates differently. Christians reckon dates from the birth of Jesus, using one of two abbreviations: B.C. (before Christ) and A.D. (Anno Domini, meaning "in the year of the Lord"); or B.C.E. (before the Common Era) and C.E. (the Common Era). Muslims count from the Hegira, Muhammad's emigration from Mecca to Medina; the era is reckoned from the first day of the year in which the Hegira took place, a date which is equivalent to July 16, 622, by Gregorian reckoning. The years are designated by the abbreviation A.H. (Anno Hegirae). Jews take as a starting point the creation of the world, estimated to have occurred in 3761/3760 B.C.E.; the customary abbreviation designating years is A.M. (Anno Mundi). An interesting note: *The Jerusalem Post,* the daily newspaper written in English, is regularly dated according to all three calendars — Christian, Jewish, and Muslim.

G. ITS POINTS OF INTEREST

Although Palestine is a relatively small country, it contains an almost unlimited number of places of interest and importance to visit. There are 5,000 sites and

The darkened "eye" in the face of this cave is Cave Four, one of several caves in which the famous Dead Sea Scrolls were found. Historians speculate that the Essenes occupied the community center at Qumran, and left these scrolls behind when they fled from the Romans.

monuments that are officially recognized — and the number is growing. In 1975, in fact, the Israeli Department of Antiquities and Museums reported the issuance of permits for 35 planned excavations and 52 emergency excavations.

Additional Reading on Life in Israel Today

Bellow, Saul. *To Jerusalem and Back.* New York: Viking Press, 1976. The Nobel Prize-winning author reports and reflects upon a large number of conversations with persons of many different political persuasions in present-day Israel. Some of the prospects envisioned are chilling.

Brilliant, Moshe. *Portrait of Israel.* New York: American Heritage Press, A New York Times Book, 1970. An account of present-day Israel by a correspondent in Israel writing for *The New York Times* and the *Times* of London, enriched by many revealing anecdotes and illustrations. A special interest guide by Sylvia R. Brilliant gives concise and precise information about particular topics, from agriculture and archeology to science and sports.

Facts about Israel. Edited by the staff of the Ministry of Information. Jerusalem, 1975. Enormously informative, in concise form.

First Fruits: A Harvest of Twenty-Five Years of Israeli Writing. Philadelphia: Jewish Publication Society, 1973. Israeli literary works.

Naamani, Israel T. *Israel: A Profile.* New York: Praeger, 1972. A discerning description.

The symbolic latticework of a window in front of the altar of the Dominus flevit Chapel frames a view of Jerusalem that includes most of the Old City. Dominating the view is the Dome of the Rock.

1. Notable Excavated Sites

Notable excavated sites of biblical importance in Palestine include Tell Dan in the far north; Hazor, overlooking the Plain of Huleh; Beth-shan, where the Valley of Jezreel meets the Valley of the Jordan; Megiddo, which controlled such a strategic pass that some of the most famous of all land battles were fought there; Jericho, which controlled the approaches to Palestine from the east; Lachish, notable from the campaigns of Sennacherib and Nebuchadnezzar II; Ashdod, one of the Philistine cities; Gezer, one of Solomon's cities (as were Hazor and Megiddo); Beersheba, on the edge of the Negev; and Qumran, where the Dead Sea Scrolls were found. These are only a few of the many noteworthy sites that can be visited.

2. Holy Places

Many sites in Palestine are shrines not only of Judaism and Christianity but also of Islam; many of these places are in fact sacred to all three of these religions. This is of course notably true of Jerusalem, often named the Holy City, and by Arab Muslims simply called al-Quds, "the Holy."

Jerusalem comprises a New City, largely in West Jerusalem, and an Old City in East Jerusalem. The site of the Old City is a roughly quadrilateral

An unmanned ladder is dwarfed by massive stones in the excavations in the Tyropoeon Valley on the west side of the Temple area. Israeli excavations have also uncovered a major approach up monumental steps to the Temple on the south, and a paved street with many shops on the west.

plateau, marked out by the Kidron Valley on the east and the Hinnom Valley on the west and south, but open to the north — the direction from which almost every conquest of the city has come. Another valley, the Tyropoeon Valley — or

---

Additional Reading on Historical Sites

Avi-Yonah, Michael, ed. *Encyclopedia of Archaeological Excavations in the Holy Land.* 2 vols. Jerusalem: The Israel Exploration Society and Massada Press, 1975-76. Detailed articles about major excavated sites.

Lapp, Paul W. "Palestine Known but Mostly Unknown." *BA,* 26 (1963), 121-134.

Negev, Avraham, ed. *Archaeological Encyclopedia of the Holy Land.* New York: Putnam, 1972. Brief articles about many sites.

Pearlman, Moshe, and Yaacov Yannai. *Historical Sites in Israel.* 2nd ed. Tel Aviv: Massadah/P.E.C. Press, 1965. Describes most of the above sites and many more of historical importance.

For information about current archeological work in Israel see the following:

Biblical Archaeologist, published quarterly by the American Schools of Oriental Research, 126 Inman St., Cambridge, MA 02139.

Biblical Archaeology Review, published monthly by the Biblical Archaeology Society, 1737 H St. NW, Washington, D.C. 20006.

Israel Exploration Journal (P.O. Box 7041, Jerusalem, Israel), a quarterly published jointly by the Israel Exploration Society, the Hebrew University Institute of Archaeology, and the Department of Antiquities and Museums of the Ministry of Education and Culture.

"Valley of the Cheesemakers," as Josephus calls it — runs diagonally through the city and divides the plateau into an eastern and a western ridge.

Across the Tyropoeon Valley to the west a portion of city wall has been found which may have been built by Hezekiah, who in the face of Assyrian threat in 701 B.C.E. dug the tunnel which runs from the Gihon Spring to the Pool of Siloam. In the first century C.E. Josephus tells of a First Wall around the main part of the city, a Second Wall around a northern suburb, and a Third Wall started by Herod Agrippa I (41-44 C.E.) and completed when the war with the Romans was imminent. The course of the Second Wall almost certainly left the site of the later Church of the Holy Sepulcher outside it; the Third Wall may have run along the course marked by the present North Wall, although some think it was located much farther to the north. The model of Jerusalem at the Holyland Hotel illustrates the course of the walls, choosing to show the Third Wall in the more northerly location.

The walls which still surround the Old City were built by Sultan Suleiman I the Magnificent from 1538 to 1542 C.E. The walls and their gates are as follows:

Eastern Wall, 762 m (2,540 ft): Golden Gate, St. Stephen's Gate
Northern Wall, 1,281 m (4,270 ft): Herod's Gate, Damascus Gate, New
    Gate
Western Wall, 875 m (2,900 ft): Jaffa Gate
Southern Wall, 1,100 m (3,700 ft): Zion Gate, Dung Gate

The earliest settlement was outside these walls on the southeastern hill above the Gihon Spring. (This conclusion is supported by the pottery found there, dating back to 3000 B.C.E. or before. Other pottery found also shows that there was settlement on the western ridge throughout Israelite history.) This was the city of the Jebusites, which King David took and made the City of David, known also as Zion (a name given later to the southwestern hill). To the north was the Temple mount, where Solomon built the Temple and his own palace.

Additional Reading on Jerusalem

Kollek, Teddy, and Moshe Pearlman. *Jerusalem: A History of Forty Centuries.* Rev. ed. New York: Random House, 1972. A handsome volume produced by the mayor of Jerusalem and an archeological writer.

Mazar, Benjamin. *The Mountain of the Lord.* Garden City: Doubleday, 1975. A most handsome volume, with details about archeological findings from the eighteenth-century excavations to modern Israeli excavations.

Shanks, Hershel. *The City of David.* Available from *The Biblical Archaeology Review,* 1737 H St. NW, Washington, D.C. 20006. A guide to earliest Jerusalem, the city of the Jebusites with their remarkable water system connected with the Gihon spring, and the city as David occupied it.

Cut into the base of this hillside are the entrances to the famous Beth Shearim catacombs. Rabbi Judah ha-Nasi made this the center of Jewish life, and was buried here when he died in about 220 C.E. His two sons and numerous other people are also buried here.

Although the Ark of the Covenant (Num. 10:33) was apparently lost and no longer available for use in the Second Temple, it remained an important symbol of the Jewish religion. Here it is represented in a carving in the Beth Shearim catacombs.

Besides Jerusalem, other holy places particularly revered by the Jews are Hebron, where Abraham purchased the cave of Machpelah; the tomb of Rachel, near Bethlehem; and Shechem, with Jacob's well and the tomb of Joseph. Holy places of later historical significance include Meron, with the tombs of Hillel and Shammai; Safad, with the tombs of the Cabalists; Tiberias, with the tombs of Yohanan ben Zakkai and others; Beth Shearim, with its catacombs; and various sites where there are ancient synagogues — Baram, high in the mountains of Upper Galilee; Capernaum, on the shore of the Sea of Galilee; and others.

The Christians revere a number of other places besides Jerusalem: Bethlehem; Nazareth; the Jordan River, where Jesus was baptized; Jericho, with the Mount of Temptation; the shores of the Sea of Galilee, with Capernaum, Peter's home, and Tabgha, traditionally thought to be the scene of the multiplication of the loaves and fishes; and Mount Tabor, believed by some to be the scene of the transfiguration.

Besides Jerusalem, places the Muslims hold sacred include Acre, with the mosque of al-Jazzar; Hattin, with the tomb of Jethro; Nebi Samwil, with the tomb of Samuel; Nebi Musa, with the tomb of Moses; and Hebron, with the mosque of Abraham.

3. Other Places to Visit

Other points of interest are virtually beyond listing, and depend to a certain extent on the visitor's personal interests. But following is at least a partial listing of intriguing places, from universities to memorials — all found in Jerusalem unless otherwise noted.

Museums: The Israel Museum, opposite the Hebrew University, which has an art museum, an archeological museum, the Shrine of the Book housing the

---

Additional Reading on Holy Places

Colbi, Saul P. *Christianity in the Holy Land, Past and Present.* Tel Aviv: Am Hassefer, 1969. In addition to the history, this work includes denominational statistics, details on ownership of the holy places, a calendar and descriptions of holyday celebrations, etc.

Finegan, Jack. *The Archeology of the New Testament: The Life of Jesus and the Early Church.* Princeton: Princeton University Press, 1969. Details archeological findings at places associated with Jesus' life, and discusses some discoveries about the early Jewish Christians.

Hollis, Christopher, and Ronald Brownrigg. *Holy Places.* New York: Praeger, 1969. Descriptions — with pictures — of Jewish, Christian, and Muslim monuments in Palestine.

Kopp, Clemens. *The Holy Places of the Gospels.* New York: Herder and Herder, 1963. English translation of the salient portions of a more detailed German work. Evaluates pilgrims' references to sacred sites.

Rosenberg, Stuart E. *Great Religions of the Holy Land.* New York: A. S. Barnes, 1971. A historical guide to sacred sites, dedicated to pilgrims of all faiths.

The Shrine of the Book at the Israel Museum is designed to provide optimum conditions for the preservation of the Dead Sea Scrolls and related materials. The top of the structure resembles the cover of the kind of jar in which the scrolls were found.

Dead Sea Scrolls, and a sculpture garden; the Palestine Archaeological Museum (the Rockefeller Museum), north of the Old City, opposite Herod's Gate, which has exhibits from the Stone Age onward; Beth Hatefutsoth, Museum of the Jewish Diaspora, Tel Aviv.

Hospitals: Hadassah-Hebrew University Medical Center, 8 km (5 mi) west of Jerusalem, overlooking the village of Ein Kerem, with a small synagogue decorated with famous stained-glass windows by Marc Chagall, each depicting one of the twelve tribes of Israel.

Universities: Hebrew University of Jerusalem; Tel Aviv University; Technion, the Israel Institute of Technology on Mount Carmel, Haifa; Weizmann Institute of Science at Rehovot, south of Tel Aviv.

Institutions of Religious and Archeological Research: Albright Institute of Archaeological Research; Dominican École Biblique; Studium Biblicum Franciscanum; Pontifical Biblical Institute; American Institute of Holy Land Studies on Mount Zion.

Artists' Colonies: Jaffa, Old City; Safad.

Music: the Israel Philharmonic Orchestra, with its permanent home in Tel Aviv; the Israel National Opera, Tel Aviv.

Theaters: the Haifa Municipal Theater; three companies in Tel Aviv: the Habiman, the Ohel, and the Kameri (Chamber) Theater.

One of the more than fifty buildings comprising Hebrew University, the Administration Building graces the campus at Givat Ram, west of Jerusalem. The school's foundation was first laid on Mt. Scopus, north of the Old City, in 1918; in 1949 the school began using improved facilities at its current location.

Memorials: Yad Vashem, west of Jerusalem, a memorial to the Jewish martyrs and heroes of the Holocaust; the John F. Kennedy Memorial, west of Jerusalem, a symbol of the close ties between Israel and the U.S.

Additional Reading on Visiting Israel

Comay, Joan. *Israel: An Uncommon Guide.* New York: Random House, 1969. The author, wife of Israel's former ambassador and permanent delegate to the United Nations, has lived in Jerusalem since the end of the Second World War. Accurate history and information, most interestingly written.

Fodor, Eugene. *Fodor's Israel.* Rev. yearly. New York: McKay. A standard guidebook, with both background articles and detailed facts for the visitor, and even an English-Hebrew vocabulary.

Vilnay, Zev. *Israel Guide.* Rev. periodically. Jerusalem: Ahiever. An excellent work on archeological and historical sites.

EPILOGUE

THE FUTURE: *A Time for Peace?*

What are the chances that Israel will become a clearly defined land, a land at peace with itself and others? The present book is intended only to carry the story up to the signing of the peace treaty between Israel and Egypt; beyond that point the events that have developed and shall develop from day to day and year to year are to be found and followed in newspapers and magazines. The future is impossible to predict, of course, but clearly it is urgently important to solve — with thoughtfulness and fairness — the problems of relationship with the Palestinians and the entire surrounding Arab and Muslim world.

That the future may be a time for peace is certainly supported by a tradition of hope. Golda Meir, for example, eloquently expressed this hope in an address she made to the eleventh session of the United Nations (on March 1, 1957) as the foreign minister of the State of Israel. She encouraged all peoples of the Middle East to work together for peace:

> We all come from an area which is a very ancient one. The hills and the valleys of the region have been witnesses to many wars and many conflicts. But that is not the only thing which characterizes that part of the world from which we come. It is also a part of the world which has given a code of ethics to all humanity. In our countries, in the entire region, all our peoples are anxious for and in need of a higher standard of living, of great programmes of development and progress.
>
> Can we, from now on — all of us — turn a new leaf and, instead of fighting with each other, can we all, united, fight poverty and disease and illiteracy? Is it possible for us to put all our efforts and all our energy into one single purpose, the betterment and progress and development of all our lands and all our peoples?

The Scriptures, too, contain similar exhortations to the people:

Pray for the peace of Jerusalem!
"May they prosper who love you!

A gift from the British Parliament, this menorah stands opposite the Knesset Building in Jerusalem as the supreme symbol of Judaism.

Peace be within your walls,
 and security within your towers!"
    (Ps. 122:6-7)

They also contain encouraging promises of peace:

"And I will appoint a place for my people Israel, and will plant them, that they may dwell in their own place, and be disturbed no more; and violent men shall waste them no more, as formerly" (I Chron. 17:9).

And with inspiring fervor Israel's national anthem — *Hatikvah* — expresses the perpetual hope of the people that this promise will be fulfilled:

So long as still within our breasts
The Jewish heart beats true,
So long as still towards the East,
To Zion, looks the Jew,
So long our hopes are not yet lost —
Two thousand years we cherished them —
To live in freedom in the Land
Of Zion and Jerusalem.